META-STUDY
OF
QUALITATIVE
HEALTH
RESEARCH

MNR
Methods in Nursing Research

SERIES EDITOR
Pamela Brink, R.N., Ph.D.

The purpose of the **Research Methods in Nursing** series is to provide basic references to designs, methods, and sampling procedures not readily available in other formats. Each book is designed to be a complete refer- ence to any single topic.

Books in This Series . . .

Ethnography in Nursing Research
Janice M. Roper
Jill Shapira

Hermeneutic Phenomenological Research
Marlene Z. Cohen
David L. Kahn
Richard H. Steeves

Meta-Study of Qualitative Health Research
Barbara L. Paterson
Sally E.Thorne
Connie Canam
Carol Jillings

META-STUDY OF QUALITATIVE HEALTH RESEARCH

A Practical Guide
to Meta-Analysis
and Meta-Synthesis

Barbara L. Paterson
Sally E. Thorne
Connie Canam
Carol Jillings

MNR
Methods in Nursing Research

Sage Publications
International Educational and Professional Publisher
Thousand Oaks ▪ London ▪ New Delhi

For information:

Sage Publications, Inc.
2455 Teller Road
Thousand Oaks, California 91320
E-mail: order@sagepub.com

Sage Publications Ltd.
6 Bonhill Street
London EC2A 4PU
United Kingdom

Sage Publications India Pvt. Ltd.
M-32 Market
Greater Kailash I
New Delhi 110 048 India

Printed in the United States of America

Library of Congress Cataloging-in-Publication Data

Meta-study of qualitative health research: A practical guide to
meta-analysis and meta-synthesis / by Barbara L. Paterson...[et al.].
    p. cm. – (Methods in nursing research; v. 3)
Includes bibliographical references and index.
    ISBN 0-7619-2414-0 (cloth: alk. paper)
    ISBN 0-7619-2415-9 (paper: alk. Paper)
    1. Meta-analysis. 2. Medicine–Research–Evaluation. I. Paterson,
Barbara L. II. Series
R853.M48 M47 2001
610'.7'2–dc21
                                    00-012991

01 02 03 04 05 06 10 9 8 7 6 5 4 3 2 1

Acquiring Editor:	Heidi Van Middlesworth
Production Editor:	Denise Santoyo
Editorial Assistant:	Candice Crosetti
Typesetter:	Barbara Burkholder
Indexer:	Teri Greenberg

CONTENTS

SERIES EDITOR'S FOREWORD

This is the third in a series of books on research methods in nursing. The purpose of the series is to provide basic references to designs, methods, and sampling procedures not readily available in other formats. The books are designed to be a complete reference to any single topic and can be used without further explanation or help from a tutor.

Nursing research has entered an era of rapidly expanding knowledge of research designs and methods suitable for answering questions of interest to the discipline. Many of these designs and data collection strategies are borrowed from other disciplines, and many of these have been altered or changed to be more useful in nursing research situations. This text falls within the general genre of an attempt to explain a method that is frequently misunderstood or misused or both.

This is a text about how to do a meta-study. Meta-studies are not for the faint-hearted and are not for the beginner; it is an advanced method to be entered into only by seasoned researchers. To do a meta-study, one must be completely familiar with the theories and research designs included in the samples. Meta-study is an in-depth analysis of published research reports on a given topic. It can be accomplished only if the research database is sufficiently large. A meta-study is a time-consuming, lengthy, scholarly process. The motivation for this kind of study is a deeply consuming need to find answers to crucial nursing questions.

For those who have had difficulty understanding the differences among meta-theory, meta-method, meta-synthesis, meta-analysis, and meta-study, we hope this text will clarify these semantic distinctions. The topic is so new that few discussions of it have been published.

—Pamela J. Brink, RN, PhD
Series Editor

PREFACE

The motivation behind this book arose from a collaborative process of investigating a human science phenomenon—the insider experience of chronic illness. As part of a team of researchers searching for methodological guidance to conduct a meta-synthesis of qualitative research on chronic illness experience, we became aware of how difficult it was to find practical and applicable information about such research approaches. At the same time, we began to recognize the excitement growing among health science researchers for the potential interpretation and application of a generation of qualitative research products. This book represents the methodological insights we have developed after several years of immersion in the complex challenges of qualitative meta-analysis and synthesis. It accounts for the processes whereby such an investigation can be conceptualized and conducted and draws from our various projects to illustrate the lessons we have learned and the convictions at which we have arrived.

Our team of researchers approached its task with established expertise in the study of specific chronic illnesses and a shared commitment to expanding knowledge on the experiences and attendant challenges of living with chronic conditions. Meta-study offered an approach for the analysis of existing reports of individual research initiatives beyond a mere aggregation of the explicit findings and into a synthesis of new knowledge that included consideration of the implication of both theory and method. From our experience, we became convinced of the potential that meta-study holds for extracting evidence from large bodies of qualitatively derived knowledge.

The research team whose methodological explorations became the foundation for this book was headed by Barbara Paterson, who served as principal investigator for the studies and principal author of this book. In addition to the three coauthors, the team involved in the meta-study projects included Dr. Sonia Acorn, Professor Gloria Joachim, and Professor Marilyn Dewis. Each colleague brought a unique theoretical and substantive slant to the project, as well as a passion for particular diseases and concepts. Working initially as a supportive colleague network within which to exchange ideas about our separate research initiatives, the team concluded that major advances in applying qualitatively derived knowledge to practice inherently depended on advances in our ability to synthesize and interpret existing bodies of research. Beginning in 1995, we launched into a series of meta-study projects. The most ambitious of these, and therefore the source of much of our experiential knowledge, was an attempt to synthesize the entire body of qualitative research into the subjective experience of chronic physical illness over the past two decades. Additional projects involved a synthesis of qualitative research into the phenomenon of adaptation to diabetes, and another synthesis of qualitative research into the phenomenon of fatigue as it is experienced across a range of chronic diseases. The knowledge we have gained from these studies, as well as the methodological insights we have obtained during the years we have been working with this method, is sufficiently complex and interesting to serve us well for the remainder of our research careers. Each of us entered the process with a decidedly naive understanding and left (if one can ever leave such work) with a changed perspective on both the complexity of the chronic illness experience and the value of knowledge synthesis.

ACKNOWLEDGMENTS

The authors gratefully acknowledge the support of coinvestigators Dr. Sonia Acorn, Marilyn Dewis, and Gloria Joachim and research funding from the Canadian Nurses Foundation.

This book is dedicated to all those with a chronic illness who, through their commitment as participants in qualitative research, have deepened and enriched health care practitioners' understanding of what it is like to live with a chronic disease.

1

INTRODUCTION

Meta-study is a research approach involving analysis of the theory, methods, and findings of qualitative research and the synthesis of these insights into new ways of thinking about phenomena. Its origins derive from the social sciences, where an earlier generation of post-positivist scholars expressed considerable interest in synthesizing diverse theoretical and disciplinary positions into grand theories (Alexander & Colomy, 1992; Ritzer, 1992a). *Meta-sociology* (Furfey, 1953) represented a systematic focus on the underpinnings, approaches, and outcomes central to sociological research. In later applications, this approach to the study of sociological theorizing was termed *meta-theorizing* (Ritzer, 1991). Within this context, *meta-study* (Zhao, 1991) was introduced as a complex and systematic approach to analyzing the existing body of sociological knowledge from several distinct perspectives. *Meta-ethnography* (Noblit & Hare, 1988) represented anthropology's attempt to synthesize and theorize its own body of research findings through a systematic cross-comparative interpretive strategy. Noblit and Hare (1988) developed meta-ethnography to identify the current understanding of a specific field of study and to raise issues for consideration in future research.

In quantitative research, especially in the health sciences, *meta-analysis* has come to represent the research strategy in which the results of numerous studies using similar instruments, data sets, and analytic methods can be reanalyzed in the aggregate (Fielding & Fielding, 1986; Glass, Smith, & McGaw, 1981). Its popularity stems from the preference for large numbers from which hypotheses can be more rigorously tested and correlations more confidently determined. The term *qualitative meta-analysis* was used first by Stern and Harris (1985) in reference to the synthesis of a group of qualitative research findings into one explanatory theory, model, or description.

It is important to clarify that, unlike some authors, we differentiate between the processes of analysis and synthesis. We believe that the findings, methods, and theory of qualitative research reports must be analyzed before a synthesis of the research can occur in order to generate new and more complete understandings of the phenomenon under study. In our use of the term *meta-study,* we extend the meta-analytic strategies developed in sociology into the domain of meta-synthesis so that the analytic sequence is directly linked to a newly synthesized research product. As a means of building generalizable knowledge from bodies of individual qualitative research reports on a particular phenomenon, meta-study offers considerable potential for application to the problems of knowledge development in the human and health sciences. In stark contrast to the traditional critical literature review that any competent researcher would complete prior to engaging in an area of study (Noblit & Hare, 1988) or to the secondary analysis of actual data sets (Thorne, 1994), meta-study represents a discrete and distinct approach to new inquiry based on a critical interpretation of existing qualitative research. It creates a mechanism by which the nature of interpretation is exposed and the meanings that extend well beyond those presented in the available body of knowledge can be generated. As such, it offers a critical, historical, and theoretical analytic approach to making sense of qualitatively derived knowledge.

In this book, we present meta-study as a systematic research process in its own right, culminating in the generation of new knowledge within a field of study. Although we do not seek to generate grand theories within the health or social sciences, we do see meta-study as being highly applicable to both a critical interpretation of the substantive contributions from various disciplines with regard to a particular phenomenon, and to developments and refinements in midrange theory about that phenomenon. Our application of meta-study research to problems associated with understanding chronic illness experience will serve as a focal lens through which the method will be illuminated, articulated, and theorized throughout the discussion. We therefore draw on our own research as a major source of examples to illustrate the many dimensions and complexities of meta-study.

CHALLENGES TO VIEWING THE INSIDER PERSPECTIVE

The importance of examining the experiences of life from the perspective of the insider—the person who is having the experience—has been increasingly recognized during the past two decades. Research of this genre, focusing on processes and issues related to health and illness, has been largely qualitative, relying primarily on in-depth, open-ended interviews with individuals who volunteer to tell an investigator about their experiences. Such research has contributed to a considerable store of qualitative work describing health and illness experiences from a subjective perspective, thus providing a rich and often revealing portrait of reactions and responses. Although a body of qualitative research exists on almost any phenomenon of interest, health care clinicians and researchers have little overall understanding of the implications of this knowledge for health care practice or for future research (Conrad, 1990; Estabrooks, Field, & Morse, 1994; Steeves, Kahn, & Cohen, 1996).

In the current era of knowledge explosion and heightened accountability to the public, it has become imperative that professional practice be based on research findings that give direction to practitioners for the most effective interventions (Sandelowski, 1997). Qualitative research from an insider perspective has been rather problematic in this regard, in that a range of methods, researcher roles, and interpretive lenses have been used to study health and illness phenomena. This issue is further complicated by some rather significant contradictions in the interpretation of findings by various qualitative researchers. For instance, the enthusiasm for advocacy among persons with HIV/AIDS has been reported by some researchers as a response to stigma (e.g., Demas, Schoenbaum, Willis, Doll, & Klein, 1995; Kendall, 1991) and by others as a normalizing strategy (e.g., Bridge, 1986; Coward & Lewis, 1993; Ragsdale, Kotarba, & Morrow, 1992). The combined problems of interpretation and generalizability make it difficult to extrapolate from individual accounts of experience to determine the contribution of a single study's findings toward applicable knowledge for understanding an individual's needs, for predicting the efficacy of various interventions, or for appreciating the implications that ought to be considered in creating appropriate health and social policy. Although each study may be interesting, informative, and thought-provoking, the body of qualitative research from the insider perspective provides many individual pieces of a jigsaw puzzle. Because researchers have little sense of what a complete picture of the phenomena of interest might eventually look like (Jensen & Allen, 1996), the relationships between these individual pieces is often difficult to imagine.

Despite a proliferation of single qualitative studies, comparative analysis of their findings and theoretical linkage of their conclusions to other relevant research have rarely been included in explorations of the insider perspective of health and illness phenomena. This trend accounts for a failure to produce midrange theory that explains and describes relationships between research findings, including those that appear at first glance to be contradictory (Statham, Mauksch, & Miller, 1988). Despite meaningful and provocative findings from individual studies, researchers have tended toward "eternally reinventing the wheel" (Sandelowski, Docherty, & Emden, 1997, p. 366) rather than capitalizing on the potential of qualitative research for developing theory and providing direction for clinical practice or policy development.

Our chronic illness research team came to realize that although much insider perspective research existed in our various substantive areas, its contribution to our practice as health care professionals was difficult to discern. We identified the need to extend the analysis of individual research studies beyond the domain of conceptualizing individual experience and to incorporate within that analysis an understanding of larger contextual issues such as dominant health system beliefs and ideologies. Although some attempts to aggregate qualitative research findings have been reported in the literature, prescriptions for conducting such syntheses, to this point, have been somewhat vague and imprecise. As Estabrooks and her colleagues (1994) point out, "the literature is . . .

virtually silent on the matter of constructing theory from multiple existing studies" (p. 504).

META-STUDY: BEYOND SYNTHESIS OF RESEARCH FINDINGS

As discussions in our research group moved beyond an initial endorsement of the need to aggregate findings in the field of chronic illness, we came to realize that merely synthesizing the results of the various available research reports was insufficient. Published syntheses in such areas as illness experience (e.g., Jensen & Allen, 1994; Morse, 1997; Morse & Johnson, 1991; Penrod & Morse, 1997) have clearly contributed to a more extensive understanding of this phenomenon. Simply combining the results of a collection of similar studies, however, excludes consideration of the highly significant ways in which theoretical, methodological, or societal contexts have shaped those reported results. As we discovered, method and theory are often inextricably linked with both data and conclusions about data. As we illustrate in the following chapters, how researchers frame chronic illness by their choice of theoretical framework influences the issues they choose to study, the questions they ask about those issues, the designs they create for the research process, their implementation of those designs, and their interpretation of the research findings. We decided that the method we used to aggregate or synthesize research would have to address all components of the research process, including theory, research methods, and data. Accordingly, we recognized that it would have to account for the historical and sociocultural factors that had shaped these components. Because our intent was to confer meaning on the findings and to construct a more extensive basis for understanding, we recognized that our method would also have to aim for interpretation and not merely the production of description of the phenomena under study. Meta-study provided a systematic means for both analyzing and synthesizing the research literature to accomplish such a goal.

As our research team conceives of it, *meta-study* refers to investigations of the results and processes of previous research (henceforth termed *primary research*). In effect, meta-study is "the research of research." It entails *analysis,* the scrutiny of the theory, method, and data analysis of research in a substantive area (Zhao, 1991), and culminates in *synthesis,* an application of that scrutiny to the generation of new knowledge. It represents an attempt not only to analyze primary research results but also to reflect on the perspectives and processes involved in those primary studies in terms of "where we are and where we are going" (Fuhrman & Snizek, 1990, p. 27). In sociology, insights gained at the level of meta-study have been acknowledged as necessary for developing an integrated canon and a practical application in social research (Bryant, 1995; Neufeld, 1994). Our research group hoped to gain similar insights into chronic illness research, with the ultimate goal of theory generation and application to practice.

In subsequent chapters of this book, we summarize the procedures and processes of meta-study as an interpretive means of both analysis and synthesis. We provide detailed guidelines for how to conduct a meta-study of qualitative research, as well as recommendations for tools and standards applicable to this research approach. Our major meta-study of qualitative research into the experience of chronic illness entailed an intensive review of 292 primary research reports culled from close to 1,000 published books, dissertations, and research articles published during a 16-year period within a range of social and health science disciplines. Examples from the chronic illness meta-study illustrate our processes, issues, and dilemmas—including the insights we gained from our own mistakes—in the hope that readers will derive some assistance in further developing and refining the methodology for their own investigations. To set the stage for a discussion of such procedures, we provide readers with a description of what we consider to be the foundational elements and components necessary to an understanding of meta-study as a unique approach to research.

PHILOSOPHICAL FOUNDATIONS OF META-STUDY

Meta-study is an interpretive qualitative research approach. Its foundations are rooted in the tenets of a constructivist orientation to epistemology and are geared toward an understanding of how individuals construct and reconstruct knowledge about a phenomenon (Denzin, 1989; Guba & Lincoln, 1994; Weinstein & Weinstein, 1992). It is important to understand that, in any meta-synthesis approach, the construction of research findings occurs at two levels: (a) The authors of primary research reports have constructed the research findings in accordance with their own understanding and interpretation of the data, and (b) the meta-synthesists have constructed an aggregated account based on their own interpretations of the primary researchers' constructions. Consequently, the meta-synthesist deals with constructions of constructions.

When we acknowledge meta-study as an interpretive constructivist approach, some underlying assumptions become apparent. First, it is accepted that no singular objective reality will be found and that multiple, coexisting, and even sometimes incongruous realities related to the phenomenon will be found instead. Therefore, prescriptions for practice, research, or theory development that are derived from meta-study research cannot be regarded as the only possible findings that could be drawn from the body of available research, but rather as those findings constructed by specific meta-synthesists at a given point in time and in accordance with their own range of interpretative skills.

Second, the primary researchers and the research subjects (variously termed *informants, participants,* or *coresearchers*) create or construct their particular understandings of the phenomenon under study. Therefore, the primary research participants construct the statements and claims that become data, the primary researchers construct findings on the basis of these data, and the meta-synthesists construct interpretations of why the primary researchers constructed findings in the way they did.

Third, constructions of the phenomenon under study are inevitably influenced by the social, cultural, and ideological contexts in which they occur. The conduct of primary research has a theoretical and historical context, and primary researchers bring their own social and political contexts to the construction of their research data. For example, as we noted in our meta-study project, primary research into chronic illness experience dating from the early 1980s was reported within an academic context in which qualitative research was relatively unusual and not well understood in many health and social science disciplines. Consequently, we located several researchers who interpreted their qualitative data by counting the frequency with which events or observations occurred, a technique that is more relevant to quantitative than to qualitative inquiries but that might have been considered more familiar by reviewers of that era.

Meta-synthesis research also occurs within a particular academic and theoretical context, and that context inevitably influences the substance and form of the interpretations. For example, we initially discounted the findings of one researcher who suggested that some people might prefer to be ill as a way of receiving attention. We believed that we could locate that particular idea in an outdated psychological interpretation of sick role behavior. In discussion, however, we came to appreciate that our rejection of those findings might have been shaped by our assumptions as health care professionals about the limitations of previous interpretations, and we came to appreciate that the contradictory ideas within the literature might help us reframe and resolve theoretical problems rather than fight against them. We have therefore come to accept that all constructions of phenomena are inherently historical and that therefore even our best understandings will always be subject to the changes that may occur over time and in different situations (Kvale, 1995). At the same time, we accept that the struggle to find more complete, relevant, and useful understandings will always be an imperative within the applied and practical disciplines.

The notion of a constructivist perspective was particularly relevant for our research group because we sought to examine critically and then reshape knowledge about facets of chronic illness. The way the assumptions underlying meta-study influenced some of our initial questions was instructive to our evolving insight about the method. Early in our project, for example, we began to detect significant differences in the way chronic illness was viewed in the 1980s as compared with the way it was viewed in reports published a decade later. In the former period, researchers tended to characterize chronic illness as a series of losses and burdens. They focused on coping with changes or deficits, such as dependency, loss of function, altered roles, and lost dreams. In the latter period, however, researchers tended to interpret chronic illness as a gift or an opportunity to view one's self in new and more meaningful ways. Researchers in the past decade have tended to emphasize positive attributes of the chronic illness experience, such as courage, transformation, and resiliency, rather than the losses and burdens associated with living with a chronic disease. Rather than conclude that the more recent researchers were more enlightened than those who had published earlier (in many cases, the authors of both kinds of reports were the same individuals), we posed questions to make sense of this evolution. We asked

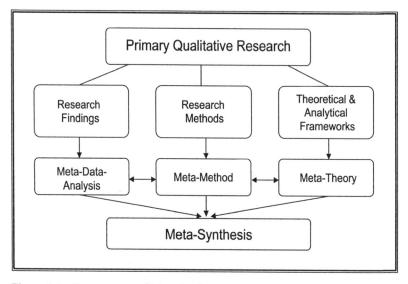

Figure 1.1. Components of Meta-Study

"Why did researchers in particular years construct the notion of chronic illness in the ways they did?" and "What historical, social, and cultural factors influenced these constructions?" A constructivist perspective allowed us to acknowledge that one group of researchers could not be seen as holding an absolute "truth" and that researchers of each era (including ourselves) were influenced by the context of the times, as well as by competing conceptualizations available in the literature to which they had access (Thorne & Paterson, 1998).

Conducting meta-study from a constructivist perspective means that the researcher functions as the interpreter of primary research reports, translating what has been written by other researchers for the purpose of revealing similarities and differences and developing theory. Translation represents the cognitive component of interpretation, wherein the researcher, as the translator, interprets the primary research findings to present the meaning of the phenomenon under study, including relationships between categories of data (Denzin, 1989). It involves making judgments about the conclusions of other researchers and extrapolating relationships among concepts, research decisions, and policy implications. Interpretation from a constructivist perspective also includes "deep, authentic understanding" (Denzin, 1989, p. 33). Authentic understanding emerges as the meta-synthesist analyzes data that align with or contradict her or his own informed assumptions about the phenomenon under study. Such an examination extends the interpretation of the cognitive material (or facts) of the research into an examination of the emotional implications (or meaning) of the data (Fuchs, 1992). It permits theorizing that accommodates previously polarized perspectives and coordinates a comprehensive understanding of complex social and human phenomena (Weinstein & Weinstein, 1992). Thus, the philosophical underpinnings of meta-study allow and, indeed, direct an attitude of openness, discovery, and reflection that is needed to discern and reframe knowledge about a particular phenomenon.

COMPONENTS OF META-STUDY

Meta-study entails analysis followed by synthesis. The analysis procedures of meta-study involve three components: meta-data-analysis, meta-method, and meta-theory. These components do not necessarily unfold sequentially and are frequently conducted concurrently. Meta-synthesis is derived from the results of the analytic components (see Figure 1.1).

Meta-data-analysis is the study of the findings of reported research in a particular substantive area of inquiry by means of processing the "processed data" (Zhao, 1991). It is an "analysis of analyses" available from reports of primary qualitative research. This process is not merely aggregative, but interpretive (Noblit & Hare, 1988), requiring researchers to examine critically multiple accounts of a phenomenon in order to reveal the similarities and discrepancies among accounts (Noblit & Hare, 1988).

Meta-method is the study of the rigor and epistemological soundness of the research methods used in the research studies. An essential component of meta-method is determining the appropriateness of particular methods in the investigation of a specific field of study (Richman, 1983). Because methodological decisions play a significant role in directing future research in a specific field of study, meta-method contributes to theory development and creates a conscious strategy for forward movement (Szmatka & Lovaglia, 1996; Szmatka, Lovaglia, & Mazur, 1996). Applying meta-method techniques to compare and contrast the findings that derive from studies using different methodological

TABLE 1.1   The Research Processes in a Meta-Study

Formulating a Research Question	• Formulating tentative question(s)
	• Choosing a theoretical framework
	• Generating workable definitions of key concepts under study
	• Anticipating outcomes of project
	• Refining the question(s)
	• Developing evaluation criteria for primary studies
Selection and Appraisal of Primary Research	• Identifying inclusion/exclusion criteria
	• Specifying appropriate data sources
	• Screening and appraisal procedure
	• Retrieving data
	• Developing filing and coding system
Meta-Data-Analysis	• Identifying analytic strategy
	• Developing filing and coding system
	• Categorizing the data
	• Obtaining intercoder consensus
	• Discussing and interpreting findings as they relate to research question(s)
Meta-Method	• Specifying methodological characteristics of selected reports
	• Elaborating on how methodological characteristics influenced research findings

Meta-Theory	• Identifying major cognitive paradigms/schools of thought that are represented in the theoretical frameworks and emerging theory of reports
	• Relating theory to larger social, historical, cultural, and political context
	• Uncovering significant assumptions underlying specific theories
Meta-Synthesis	• Critically interpreting the strengths and limitations of the various discrete contributions to the field
	• Uncovering significant assumptions underlying specific theories
	• Searching for alternative explanations for paradoxes and contradictions within the field
	• Determining which existing theoretical stances are and are not compatible and why
	• Proposing alternative theoretical structures within which existing knowledge can be interpreted
Disseminating the Findings	• Determining appropriate audiences
	• Determining appropriate vehicles for dissemination of findings
	• Writing and presenting the findings

researchers, we know much more about the field, including the contributions of our own research, and we appreciate the implications of qualitative methodological decisions at a much deeper level than we did before. Perhaps just as important, we have had a great deal of fun.

2

LAYING THE GROUNDWORK
FOR META-STUDY

Beginning a meta-study project is similar to beginning any major research endeavor in that it typically entails weeks, if not months, of preparatory work. The initial steps include establishing the research team and determining (and agreeing on!) the purpose of the meta- study. The research question that will guide the entire project can then be formulated and a theoretical framework selected. Finally, application for funding can be considered.

ESTABLISHING THE RESEARCH TEAM

We consider meta-study to be a team effort, rather than an individual enterprise, because the nature of the research involves the inherent problems of multiple perspectives and reflection about them. Within a team in which various opinions are celebrated, consultation, clarification, and confirmation by others counters the challenge of individual "stuck-points" and biases (Erlandson, Harris, Skipper, & Allen, 1993). Although all teamwork in qualitative research relies on regular consultation among team members, an ongoing commitment to systematic consultation processes is probably even more crucial in a meta-study project, which may involve keeping track of as many as several hundred primary research reports.

As we illustrate later in the book, in the process of meta-study many decisions are made; the differing opinions of team members concerning these decision will become an important source of insight about subtle distinctions and variations within primary research that will eventually inform the meta-study findings. In our project, for example, we determined that crucial decisions, such as the research studies to be included and appraisal of the findings, method, and theory, would require agreement by at least three team members. When we encountered split opinions, we discussed the issue as a group. Each of these discussions led to a general refinement of our collective understanding of how we would proceed and why and engaged our thinking in the larger objectives of the project.

Meta-study also requires a vast array of methodological, content, and theoretical knowledge (Schreiber, Crooks, & Stern, 1997). Generally, one person is unable to claim expertise in all areas. Our research teams have involved up to seven researchers with specific expertise in various substantive knowledge areas and methodological approaches. All have been primary investigators on funded projects whose results have been published in peer-reviewed journals, and several have also written about qualitative research methods.

Having too many researchers on a meta-study research team may be just as problematic as having too few. If the research team is too large, effective communication can be cumbersome, and collaboration about significant decisions may become difficult or even impossible.

Meta-study research team members should

- Be experienced in conducting and analyzing qualitative research (Estabrooks et al., 1994)

- Be skilled in content flexibility, inductive reasoning, and theory analysis and have the ability to transform ideas across levels of abstraction (Burns, 1989)

- Share a common interest in the research area

- Have the time, energy, and commitment to pursue the taxing demands of the meta-study

We attribute the success of our chronic illness meta-study venture to the fact that our research team members knew each other and had read each other's work prior to the meta-study. We worked well together and respected and enjoyed one another. Further, we held similar ideas about research and shared a common set of values about how research teams should operate.

Because meta-study is a significant investment and requires considerable commitment on the part of a team, we suggest that those considering joining such a project attempt to clarify what they are willing to contribute and what they expect to gain from participation. The following set of questions, asked individually or collectively, may be helpful in guiding this reflective process:

- For what purpose(s) is the meta-study being conducted?
- Who will be the intended audience of the meta-study findings?
- Who will be able to use the products of the meta-study?
- Do the researchers have the necessary resources to access primary research reports in their own discipline or country? In other disciplines and countries as well as their own?
- Do the researchers have sufficient time, space, and expertise to conduct the meta-study?
- Who are the other members of the research team, and how were they selected?
- How will the team members relate to and interact with one another? What will be the role of the principal investigator or project manager?
- How will conflicts and differing points of view be resolved within the research team?

COLLABORATION AMONG TEAM MEMBERS

The real benefits of collaborative team research in meta-study are obtained when the relationships among the researchers are characterized by frank, open discussions of expectations, needs, and goals. Collaboration allows all researchers to maximize their personal strengths in the research process and to learn from the abilities and experience of the others. A major challenge associated with being a member of a collaborative research team is that it is typically more time-consuming than

our research in the area of chronic illness. Several of us were frustrated with the ambiguity and contradiction that existed within this body of research in general and as it related to our own specific concerns about the experience of living with a chronic illness. We soon discovered that we shared a vision to go beyond individual research accounts, to create an integrated body of knowledge related to the experience of living with chronic illness, and in so doing, to advance the field of study.

"Meta-study starts with an examination of problems encountered in primary study and ends with prescriptions for resolving these problems" (Zhao, 1991, p. 381). It may also arise from a desire to make sense of a large body of research that appears to have no apparent framework and that has remained largely unexamined by others. With discussion, reflection, and revision, general aims and objectives become more explicit and purposeful. Careful attention to the processes of clarifying and narrowing your purpose at this stage enhances the direction of all subsequent steps in the research.

We discovered that it is especially helpful to imagine the outcomes of the meta-study at the beginning of the project. Projecting what one wishes to occur as a result of the meta-study (e.g., developing a model or framework related to the research topic, critiquing the research methods used to date) assists in refining the purpose and gives direction to formulating the research question. One of our goals for the chronic illness meta-study, for example, was to determine why some people find meaning and hope in living with chronic illness and others do not. This goal helped in shaping a methodological decision, in that we knew we would have to include studies in which the researchers investigated such concepts as meaning, coping, hope, transcendence, spirituality, and adaptation. We also knew that our research question would have to recognize breadth in the field while also being sufficiently focused to direct us to primary research that could result in such an outcome.

FORMULATING A RESEARCH QUESTION

The meta-study research question may pertain to a broad or narrow construct or phenomenon. Choosing a broad focus has the advantage of allowing a focus on the overall construct, as well as on related phenomena. Choosing a narrow focus has the advantage of limiting the breadth of available research the team will be able to consider. The research question should be broad enough to capture the attributes of the phenomenon under study in various contexts and situations but narrow enough to create a feasible limit to the number of primary research reports to be included. The breadth and nature of the research question should reflect the extent of the research to be aggregated, as well as the concepts and themes to be examined. The initial research question guiding our chronic illness meta-study was "What does the body of qualitative research pertaining to the experience of chronic illness from the perspective of the insider tell us about the nature of that experience?" We quickly discovered that this question was too broad and did not provide sufficient direction for the sampling primary research studies to be included in our meta-study. Because of the extensive body of qualitative research about chronic illness, we determined to limit our scope to the perceptions of adults with chronic illness from their perspective as insiders, rather than the explicit perspectives of their family members or health care professionals. Furthermore, our initial question did not provide any direction to our definition of chronic illness or to our theoretical orientation to the phenomenon. Consequently, we refined the initial question and asked "What is the experience of adults who live with a chronic illness in terms of the impact of the illness on the individual's life and his or her ability to adapt to and manage the illness?"

SELECTING A THEORETICAL FRAMEWORK

The articulation of a theoretical framework is significant in a meta-study because it assists the researcher(s) in defining the relevant concepts and constructs in the research question, directing the sampling procedures, and determining the basis for the interpretation of the findings. Because adopting an existing framework from among the theoretical perspectives available in the literature may inject a particular bias into the meta-study, many researchers may find it more helpful to draw on such work when reflecting on their options for defining terms and for articulating the nature and boundaries of the phenomena under study. Thus, when we refer to this theoretical framework, we are referring to a coherent set of claims that will provide direction throughout all phases of the study. Without any such framework, the researcher is likely to become immobilized in the complexity of clarifying the domain and making somewhat arbitrary decisions along the way. Thus, a theoretical framework provides defined limits to what meta-study researchers want to examine within the energy, resource, and time restrictions under which they must necessarily operate.

In articulating a framework, the researcher "unmasks" the various conceptualizations and interpretations that will inevitably contribute to any qualitative enterprise (Sandelowski, 1993b). A useful theoretical framework should contribute to a definition of the phenomenon of study that is broad enough to capture the variations in interpretation by researchers but narrow enough to provide boundaries and direction to literature retrieval. It should provide a mechanism with which the meta-synthesist can comfortably reconcile variations in the definition and level of abstraction of concepts as they are employed in the primary studies. In our chronic illness meta-study, we worked from a model of chronic illness devised by Curtin and Lubkin (1990) as our theoretical framework because it clearly explains the experience of living with a chronic illness as entailing both the impact of the illness on the individual and/or significant others, as well as adaptation to and management of the disease. This clarity helped us provide an operational and conceptual definition of the topic of our study; that is, it enabled us to define what we did and did not mean when we used the term *chronic illness*. For example, we did not include blindness as a chronic illness because it did not require ongoing "medicosocial intervention" (Curtin & Lubkin, 1990, p. 18). It also assisted us in defining the relevant concepts and constructs that would be included in the meta-study, as well as in developing a list of terms to use for locating research that pertained to the experience of living with a chronic illness. For example, it helped us in framing the decision to include primary research in which the focus of the research was such various issues as the quality of life, the financial impact of the illness, and the learning that was required to manage the disease.

Although the choice of a theoretical framework for a meta-study project directs the research design, it can also lead to ambiguity and uncertainty, which in turn leads researchers to question their basic assumptions about the field of study. To illustrate, we noted that disability is part of the conceptualization of chronic illness developed by Curtin and Lubkin (1990). This required that we include primary research about disability in the meta-study. At times, this inclusion caused us concern. We revisited the decision to include disability on several occasions. Our hesitation about including studies about disability was that to do so implied that disability was an illness. In contrast, because mental illness is not part of Curtin and Lubkin's framework, we did not include it in our theoretical definition of chronic illness. We were challenged to reconsider this decision as the project unfolded, however, because we soon discovered that the boundaries between mental and physical chronic illness are fuzzy and that much of the research-based knowledge that is related to chronic physical chronic illness has significant application to chronic mental illness. Indeed, our meta-study process led us to rethink the basis for distinguishing between the two in health and social science research. Thus, an unexpected outcome of our chronic illness meta-study was that we now have research-based evidence to refute and clarify the implications of the theoretical framework we chose. For example, we can now present a much more confident theoretical claim to distinguish between the experience of someone who has a chronic illness such as diabetes and another who has a nonprogressive disability sustained as a result of injury.

OBTAINING FUNDING

Some granting agencies welcome meta-study research proposals because of the promised outcomes of such research, particularly in the area of health and social policy. Meta-study research teams have no difficulty responding to the stipulation of some granting agencies that funding is given only to those who establish extensive collaborative networks. The outcomes of meta-study are so varied that they can be tailored to meet the mandate of a granting agency. Granting agencies that emphasize clinical application of research will respond favorably to a meta-study that will result in the identification of constructive interventions. Penrod and Morse (1997), for example, conducted a meta-synthesis of the findings of qualitative research studies about hope in illness. They developed a framework for assessing hope in clients. Granting agencies that focus on health policy or population-based care will accept meta-study research proposals in which the researchers propose to determine health or social policy implications for a specific population.

However, some granting agencies not yet familiar with the benefits of this kind of research may require arguments convincing enough to modify their existing funding policies.

Here are a few suggestions for increasing the likelihood of getting your meta-study research proposal funded:

1. *Do not assume that the proposal reviewers will understand meta-study.* Include clear directions about what meta-study is, how it was developed, and how it has been used in the past to generate specific outcomes. You may want to explain how meta-study is related to, but different from, such approaches as meta-analysis or conventional meta-synthesis.

2. *Conduct a preliminary review of the relevant research prior to writing the proposal.* Let the reviewers know the anticipated range of qualitative research available to you. Write about this range in terms of numbers (e.g., "More than 300 such studies are listed in CINAHL") and in terms of the nature of this research (e.g., "Although numerous studies are available in the area of decision making in illness, fewer than 20 studies were located that dealt specifically with the everyday decision making involved in chronic illness self-management").

3. *Be aware of and cite in your proposal any literature reviews that focus on a similar area.* Identify why you think a meta-study of this body of research will contribute more to, and generate new insights beyond, the literature syntheses. For example, we were aware that several reviews of chronic illness research had been conducted by several authors. In our grant proposal, we stated that these reviewers had focused on a specific construct rather than on the totality of the chronic illness experience. We also pointed out that they had not differentiated between the disease-specific aspects of the experience of living with a chronic illness and had not clarified the relationship between relevant constructs in the field.

4. *Allow for sufficient funds to cover the expenditures in the meta-study.* The major costs associated with a meta-study project involve obtaining primary research reports and paying the salaries of any secretarial supports, research assistants, or project managers.

5. *Identify clearly the procedures you will use in the meta-study, citing examples of how they have been used in other research or disciplines.* For example, in our proposal to conduct the chronic illness

meta-study, we cited several examples of how sociologists used the procedures of meta-theory to analyze sociological theory.

6. *If you are asked to suggest reviewers for the proposal, select people who have actually conducted such research.* Although many authors have written about meta-synthesis of qualitative research, few have actually conducted a project of this nature. Not all reviewers are familiar with meta-study, and those who have conducted similar research are likely to understand and provide support for aspects of the proposal that may be puzzling to others. For example, the proposed timeline of meta-study research may look prolonged to someone who has never conducted meta-study research, but a reviewer who has done so will know that it takes weeks, and sometimes months, for some primary research reports to arrive from other countries.

7. *If this is your first meta-study research project, consider conducting a small meta-study of an aspect of the larger phenomenon you propose to study; this will serve as a pilot test of the meta-study.* For example, if you intend to conduct a meta-study of fatigue in illness, conduct a meta-study of 10 grounded theory research reports about fatigue that arises from dyspnea in chronic illness. Cite this pilot test throughout the proposal (e.g., "The budget costs for document retrieval have been based on costs incurred for the retrieval of the eight articles and two dissertations in the meta-study pilot"). Be sure to identify any difficulties or surprises you encountered in the pilot and what you intend to change in the larger meta-study because of these insights.

8. *Although ethical considerations are minimal in such a project because human subjects are not involved, you need to include in the proposal a statement indicating that you know this to be so and that you recognize an ethical responsibility to indicate the primary research sources in any publication arising from the meta-study. Reviewers who are not familiar with the method may need the rationale for why you did not apply for ethical review of the proposed research.*

LESSONS LEARNED

In proposing our original chronic illness meta-study project, we made some mistakes from which we learned a great deal. We offer them to you to help you in planning for predictable challenges when you write a meta-study research proposal. We thought, for example, that our large meta-study project would easily be completed within a year. In fact, it took 30 months to achieve a beginning meta-synthesis, and it may take a lifetime to integrate fully all aspects of the venture. We failed to consider the significant time it would take to retrieve relevant research reports and to coordinate a systematic review of those reports. In some ways, a meta-study can never be considered entirely completed. As you progress in a meta-study project, you will discover questions raised about the phenomenon under study that you had not anticipated when you wrote the proposal. Because granting agencies need to know that the research will be finished and disseminated within a specific period of time, we suggest that you anticipate a typical meta-study may require 18 months to retrieve, appraise, analyze, and enter data for 100 primary research reports, for example, and an additional 6 months to synthesize and write the final report. The time required to review primary research reports can be decreased considerably if you have more than one team of reviewers and a systematic process in place. We had two teams to review primary research reports and consequently finished the full appraisal and analysis of 292 reports in 2 years.

Another mistake we made was to assume that we could conduct the research without the benefit of a project manager. Recognizing the extent to which we would have to immerse ourselves in the work to conduct the meta-study project, we assumed that all the technical aspects of coordinating meetings and retrieving and filing documents would be easily managed by the investigators themselves. Further, because we believed in a cooperative effort, we assumed that we could effectively apportion the administrative activities equally and still keep track of our processes and procedures. In time, the principal investigator was forced to assume the role of project manager as well, and we became convinced that having one "boss" was critical to managing the flow of processes, paperwork, and activities.

One of the most time-consuming exercises was arranging team meetings. Coordinating the schedules of seven very busy academics to communicate the meta-study findings and to make decisions was not a simple undertaking. It often took several telephone calls, e-mails, and cancellations before a meeting took place. We found it best to have whole-day meetings on weekends, as it was difficult to find even an hour or two during a workweek that were free for everyone on the team. Another difficulty was that the team members really enjoyed each other's friend-ship; the meetings represented one of the few times that we were able to visit with one another, and the early part of each meeting was often spent catching up on news and events. By the end of the project, we had learned to plan our meetings several weeks in advance and to allocate time for socialization apart from the agenda of the meta-study.

We had also not anticipated the amount of space that such a project might require. Our offices began to overflow with the paper that re-sulted from copies of the primary research reports, the researchers' re-views, the minutes of our research team meetings, and relevant litera-ture to support the components of the meta-study. Within 6 months of the initiation of the study, we had to request an additional office for the filing of reports, as well as for accommodating data entry by our re-search assistants. We had to develop effective tracking systems for those items that could be removed from the office and those that could not and mechanisms for determining who had what resources at any one point in time. Although we had originally intended that a single copy of most primary research reports could be shared within the team, we found that limiting the time each member could immerse in the reports detracted from the quality of our analyses; so, we created a system in which multiple copies of reports could be in circulation at any one time.

We also underestimated the cost of including dissertations in our chronic illness meta-study. Many universities no longer send disserta-tions via interlibrary loans. Because these must be purchased as hard copies or as microfiche, they can be quite expensive. But because they often represent cutting edge research and provide considerably more detail than the typical research paper, we found them indispensable. An-other unexpected cost factor was the sheer volume of photocopying re-quired. Because we had assumed that effective systems for sharing single copies of reports would suffice, we discovered that we had grossly un-derestimated the photocopy costs for the project and had to accommo-date some additional photocopy expenses out-of-pocket.

Finally, we also failed to anticipate how attractive a "ready-made" bibliography could be to students, colleagues, and others working in the field of chronic illness. Because we had access to computer files from which a collection of all qualitative research on a particular disease could be easily extracted and a filing cabinet with copies of the original research reports, we were soon inundated with requests to share our materials with other researchers. This posed both ethical and practical dilemmas for our team. Recognizing the logic and rationale for our own selection criteria, we came to believe that granting access to our files might be problematic for the comprehensiveness of literature reviews for other purposes. Further, as documents started to go missing from our files, we began to recognize the problems associated with a lightly controlled access system. These difficulties led us to some thoughtful conversations about even our own current and future uses of the database, because most members of our team continue to do research in relation to various chronic illness issues and will, from time to time, find the database an excellent beginning point for considering new questions.

CONCLUSION

Conducting a meta-study involves steps similar to those of any other research project. You begin by articulating the purpose, formulating a research question based on that purpose, and defining the theoretical boundaries you will use to constrain the concepts and constructs under study. You also identify potential funding sources, develop a proposal, and build a budget based on your understanding of the various activities and procedures involved.

Meta-study departs from many other research approaches in its inherent dependence on a team effort. Because ongoing collaboration and consultation among team members are a crucial aspect of any meta-study, it is imperative that time be devoted to establishing working strategies among the team members. Extensive preparation will help make the demands of the meta-study project more concrete at the outset, increase the credibility of the proposed research to funding agencies, and eliminate many predictable problems that can otherwise occur in meta-study research.

3

THE RETRIEVAL AND ASSESSMENT
OF PRIMARY RESEARCH

Perhaps the most significant aspect of determining the quality of meta-study research is obtaining the actual primary research reports you will rely on to describe the phenomenon under study. This is not as easy as it appears at first blush. Numerous decisions must be made about what primary research is or is not appropriate to include in a meta-study. In addition, there are the difficulties in accessing all the possible primary research reports that could be included in the meta-study. Because the quality of the product is dependent on the quality of the data, careful attention to the retrieval process is crucial to the success of the meta-study.

RETRIEVAL OF PRIMARY RESEARCH REPORTS

Primary research studies in a meta-study project may be located in several sources. These include computer searches (e.g., CINAHL, PsychLIT, SocioFile, MEDLINE), abstracting services, citation indexes to identify relevant research reports, reference lists at the conclusion of research reports, research reports and other relevant publications, and professional and journal networks to obtain unpublished studies (Cooper, 1982, 1987; Onyskiw, 1996). Generally, meta-synthesists use an average of six or seven techniques to locate primary research studies; the most popular approaches are examination of past reviews and computer searches of reference databases (Cooper & Lindsay, 1998). As Internet, technological search, and collegial networking options advance, however, researchers will undoubtedly be increasingly creative in this aspect of the investigation.

Different research sources will create subtle differences in the actual material that will be identified and retrieved. Reference databases, for example, often include research that is limited to certain publication sources and types of research report. In determining the quality of the retrieval from any one source, it is important to understand its own acceptance or inclusion criteria. Many available databases exclude research from certain countries, published in certain languages. In our chronic illness meta-study, we obtained primary research reports from North American countries, Thailand, Australia, New Zealand, the Scandinavian countries, and the United Kingdom. We found it much more difficult to locate research originating from South American countries, Korea, India, and several other countries in which we know of researchers who conduct such research. Further, because qualitative research often spans the social and health sciences, many databases reflect only the contributions of certain disciplines. Others are highly restrictive in what journals they index and therefore will give a distorted portrait of the available research. An example is MEDLINE, which failed to index papers from the journal *Qualitative Health Research* for a decade after it began publication. Beyond the most obvious databases, we found professional computer discussion groups and networks (e.g., Nursenet) to provide a valuable collateral source for such research. We have also learned how to use the Internet to contact individual professionals, academic departments, and professional associations for information about accessing relevant research in countries in which the results may not have been published or indexed in the more widely accessible formats.

Meta-study researchers can also obtain data from part of a primary research report if those data are clearly demarcated. Some of the primary research studies we reviewed in our chronic illness meta-study had both qualitative and quantitative components. Others had one component dealing with the individual with chronic illness and another addressing family caregivers. We included these reports where we could easily distinguish or detach the relevant aspects of the report from those that would not otherwise have fit our inclusion criteria. Where the results were sufficiently integrated that the source of ideas was not easily distinguishable, we did not include them. Recognizing that potentially useful primary reports may be indexed or categorized in various ways (e.g., being recorded as descriptive studies rather than as qualitative research), we would discourage any retrieval system that is overly reliant on predetermined indexing systems.

A common source of researcher bias related to all forms of research literature synthesis is the omission of relevant reports (Cook & Leviton, 1980). Gaps in awareness about what has been investigated and reported in a meta-study may therefore result in a highly limited capacity to approach midrange theory because the eventual quality of the meta-study depends on comprehension of all the primary research available. Despite one's best efforts to locate primary research appropriate to a research question, it is extremely difficult, if not impossible, to locate all primary research within a specific field of study (Cooper & Lindsay, 1998). At best, the researcher is likely to capture only a representative sample of the available research in a particular area of study. Even after several years of exhaustive searching by a large team of researchers using multiple strategies, we continue to identify chronic illness primary research reports we might have included had we located them during our project. Indeed, we have sometimes been quite surprised to notice what is missed through reliance on computer searches and consultation with professional networks. This problem illustrates the importance of documenting both the processes and the actual research reports included in the meta-study so that others can judge the breadth of the data retrieval. If retrieval efforts are diligent, researchers cannot be faulted for the obscure articles and reports that might escape their notice and therefore be missed in the final analysis (Cooper & Lindsay, 1998). The importance of familiarity with the characteristics and nature of the body of literature cannot be underestimated, however, and so meta-study is a method best reserved for those with preexisting comfort in their fields.

The meta-study researcher must decide whether to include unpublished as well as published primary research reports. An argument in support of including only published reports is that the publication process becomes a device for screening and maintaining the quality of research reports (Cooper & Lindsay, 1998), especially in a blind-peer-reviewed journal. We have concluded, however, that the range in the quality, scope, and depth of published works is considerable, even within the top-ranked scholarly journals. Depending on a range of factors, including the publication standards of the era, the formatting requirements and space limitations of the journal, and the perceived expectations of the intended audience, published studies may or may not appear as top-quality reports. Some publications are missing pertinent data or significant aspects of the research design; others are exemplary in detail and comprehensiveness. Thus, we believe that criteria other than acceptance for publication are appropriate for optimal meta-study retrieval strategies.

Estabrooks and colleagues (1994) have noted that dissertations and theses are most appropriate in a meta-study because they must adhere to the standards of academic rigor required by universities, whereas published reports may be more specifically shaped by editorial policy. We have found that dissertations are often particularly useful in providing a more detailed appreciation for what was done in the research and how conclusions were derived. In fact, in comparing what we have gleaned from several dissertations in comparison with the formal publications that arose from them, we have often been struck by how different a study's findings can appear when they are reduced to a more tightly constructed message, such as can be reported in 15 manuscript pages. However, including unpublished primary reports in a meta-study also has significant limitations. Often, these reports are difficult to access because they are not included in computerized literature databases and are generally not in the public domain. Thus, it is difficult to determine with any confidence how effectively you have sampled the total available population of such studies. It is also more difficult to establish an audit trail of your logic when readers may not have access to the same resources. As has already been mentioned, another relevant issue is the cost of retrieval of unpublished research. Because such research typically cannot be borrowed but must be purchased, meta-study researchers must make judgments about its likely inclusion even prior to initial view; this can create quite different inclusion and exclusion processes for various kinds of primary research. Unlike published research, in which you can quite often track the nature of what was excluded, you are not likely to invest in a report without a reasonable degree of certainty that it will be relevant.

In our meta-study of chronic illness experience, we chose not to include master's theses beyond those located in the Canadian Nurses Association library because it was difficult even to identify what might be available, let alone locate it. Although we were well aware that many of these studies would have added to the breadth and richness of the meta-study, listings of master's theses are not currently available on computerized literature databases or in *Dissertation Abstracts International*. The only way of obtaining a comprehensive listing of master's theses would be to contact each university library directly. We therefore regretfully concluded that this task would be too time and energy intensive to warrant their inclusion. As indexing systems improve, this potential data source may also become more accessible.

If the volume of primary research reports used in a meta-study is too great, data analysis becomes too cumbersome to permit anything but gross generalizations without appropriate depth and breadth. If the volume is too small, the credibility and trustworthiness of the meta-study findings will be jeopardized. It is important, then, to consider the question, How many retrieved reports are necessary to address the research question effectively in a meta-study? Although this question has no definitive answer, a reasonable approach will depend on an understanding of the context, the question, and the state of the art as far as knowledge development has taken us. In general, the following principles should be considered in determining the sample size that will be appropriate for your meta-study project:

- The data should be sufficient to permit comparisons among selected dimensions and constructs.

- The reports should reflect the work of several distinct and independent investigators.

- The data should be sufficient to answer the research question(s) fully.

In many instances, an iterative process between reflection on the research question and determination of the potentially available set of primary research reports will help in clarifying which questions can be answered by using meta-study and which cannot. If only a handful of primary research reports are involved or if they reflect research in a specific discipline, era, or project, meta-study would most likely only serve to re-create whatever flaws or biases exist in the original research. In such cases, broadening the question might allow for a more satisfactory investigation. For example, when she discovered that there were too few studies of the subjective impact of dance therapy on geriatric populations, one researcher chose to broaden her investigation to include consideration of all sensory and creative approaches to that population. If the body of research in a field is vast, such that it will be difficult to exclude any primary studies, a refinement of the research question may be in order. For example, our original, very broad chronic illness research question that yielded almost 300 research reports was much too loose to produce useful findings. Over time, as that project evolved, we found it necessary to articulate narrower questions and subsequently to work with subsets of the total database to create convincing conclusions about certain kinds of phenomena. Thus, although a specific target number may not be appropriate, we would generally recommend that at least a dozen discrete studies be available from which to work to make meta-study meaningful and that working with data sets of more than 100 primary research reports may be overly ambitious for most investigators.

A final issue we would like to mention also arose in our chronic illness meta-study and has continued to be a perplexing challenge in our subsequent projects. It involves the difficulty of determining which published reports represent discrete accounts of distinct studies and which actually represent duplicate publications or minor variations on previous reports of the same study. For example, although it might be anticipated that aspects of dissertation research would be subsequently published in journal articles, some authors failed to refer to their dissertations, and so it was not clear whether a report represented further investigation. In other instances, two apparently distinct research reports by a single author or group might claim to answer different research questions and report significantly different interpretations of findings; however, subtle cues in the timing, demographic makeup, or verbatim quotations of the research participants might suggest that a report was either a different spin on the original research or an unstated secondary analysis. In writing up our meta-study reports, therefore, we report both the total number of primary research studies we have reviewed and the number of those that appear to represent discrete research projects.

CRITERIA FOR INCLUSION

Because multiple research reports may be available on any particular subject, meta-study researchers must be clear about the nature of the reports they require in order to address the research question. This task entails deciding on the criteria for selection of primary research. Some aspects to be included in selection criteria are the nature of the study population (e.g., adults, persons of color), the timeline of reporting (e.g., the date of publication, the dates during which the research was conducted), the nature of the disciplines to be represented (e.g., nurse-authored only, from all health care professions), and any relevant methodological characteristics. The selection criteria for our chronic illness meta-study project included the following types of research reports:

- Reports written by nurses, physicians, social scientists or allied health professionals
- Reports in which the participants were individuals or aggregates with a diagnosis of a chronic illness, excluding those with a primary chronic mental illness
- Reports identifiable as a qualitative research investigation in which the researcher(s) investigated the experience of living with a chronic illness from the perspective of the individual with the disease
- Reports published between January 1980 and July 1995 in a refereed journal, monograph, anthology, or doctoral dissertation
- Reports that provided sufficient evidence of a data trail to demonstrate how the data were analyzed
- Reports that provided a demographic profile of participants

Among the many challenges in the use of meta-study is determining the fit between the purpose of the meta-study and that of the primary research studies on which it is based. If the research questions differ dramatically in the primary research study and the meta-study, the primary study may offer little to the purposes of the meta-study. In the chronic illness meta-study, for example, we encountered research reports in which the researchers claimed a focus on the experience of living with a chronic illness but actually restricted their interpretation to an isolated concept such as hope or spirituality. In such instances, the description of participants' perceptions regarding the concept took precedence in the report and may not have even been considered in the context of any larger questions about what it was like to live with a chronic illness. In time, we found that we could be comfortable including such studies because we had confidence that their contributions could be interpreted within the meta-theory phase of analysis.

Different criteria for primary research selection are appropriate for different research questions and different research approaches (Sandelowski et al., 1997). For example, if the meta-study question seeks clarification of the influence of the researcher's gender on participants' responses, the criteria by which a relevant study would be determined would have to include consideration of the researcher's involvement with the participants. In our chronic illness meta-study, we recognized the importance of being able to identify in the report the nature of the sample from which the researchers' interpretations were drawn. For example, indications of the participants' ages, gender, ethnicity, level of education, and specific chronic diseases were all instructive to our interpretive process and enabled us to make the kinds of cross-group comparisons that were necessary to answer our research questions effectively.

Considerable debate surrounds the question whether one can use studies representing primary reports that use different qualitative research methods in a meta-synthesis project. Some argue that differing qualitative methods should not be combined because of the differing assumptions about reality that underpin each method (Jensen & Allen, 1994, 1996; Sherwood, 1999). The social process emphasis of grounded theory, for example, would be expected to produce different data than would the more subjective focus of a phenomenological study. Jensen and Allen (1996) propose that one danger of blending qualitative approaches is that this may complicate the meta-synthesis with substantively different kinds of knowledge that cannot be translated into one another. Others (e.g., Knafl & Breitmayer, 1991; Miles & Huberman, 1994; Stern, 1994) believe that including research that uses different qualitative methods contributes to the depth and breadth of the description of the phenomenon under study and counterbalances the strengths and limitations of individual methods.

Although this issue is discarded as a moot point by some (e.g., Kavale & Glass, 1981), others state that such an "apples and oranges" treatment in aggregation research is likely to produce invalid findings (Onyskiw,

1996). This issue is further complicated by the fact that studies claiming discrete methodological orientations can appear remarkably similar in their approaches, whereas others locating themselves in the same qualitative approach can differ dramatically (Sandelowski et al., 1997). Depending on the genealogical tradition that a grounded theorist ascribes to, for example, the language, syntax, conceptual structure, and presentation style may be quite different from those used in reports in which the researcher locates him- or herself in another "camp" within the method.

If primary research reports are regarded as the sample of the meta-study, they can vary in characteristics as would the sample of participants in an individual research study. We agree that the epistemological approach must be generally consistent with the notion of insider perspectives and constructed understandings. In our meta-study, we often found discrepancies in what primary researchers identified as their research method and what they described as their approach to the study. We often found evidence that they applied methodological traditions not indicated by the method they claimed they used (e.g., grounded theories about lived experience). In the earlier years and in particular journals and disciplines, qualitative research was characterized by lack of detail regarding data collection and analysis and often included some practices that might no longer be considered consistent with qualitative strategies (e.g., counting all the times specific data events occurred and attempting to draw correlations between data components).

We believe that much of the debate just described can be explained by the current embryonic state of qualitative meta-synthesis approaches. Many of those arguing against inclusion of different kinds of research do so because their synthesis strategies rely entirely on aggregating findings of similar kinds of studies and because they have no analytic mechanism by which to capitalize on the implications of variations within the larger body of research-based knowledge. As we explain in detail in Chapter 7, we believe that building meta-synthesis on an explicit basis of meta-data-analysis, meta-method, and meta-theory is what makes meta-study so much more intriguing and complex than the more aggregative meta-synthesis approaches. In our work, we include the fullest possible range of research methods and theoretical approaches so that we can use the meta-study process to identify and make sense of methodological incongruities, rather than exclude them from our analysis.

Another decision we have made in our work is to seek out primary research reports in which the researchers use strategies congruent with an interpretivist epistemological stance, regardless of whether or not they have acknowledged that tradition. Taking an extreme position on this matter, one researcher has argued the legitimacy of including both qualitative and quantitative research in a meta-synthesis on the basis that each reveals different aspects of a phenomenon under study (Heyman, 1996). She combined one qualitative study with four quantitative research reports concerning the experience of diabetes management to conduct a meta-analysis of the findings. We would not advocate such an approach in meta-study because of the radically differing views of knowledge that are fundamental to qualitative and quantitative approaches. We would agree with Sandelowski (1986), however, that the differentiation between quantitative and qualitative research is not always as clear as most researchers contend. In some instances, for example, researchers use some quantitative data as a device to legitimate their research but the thrust of their report is decidedly constructivist, interpretive, and inductive. We believe that this kind of approach is consistent with an orientation toward inquiry that attempts to understand the meaning of a situation or phenomenon through the interpretations of those who live it; we would be favorably inclined to consider including such primary reports in our meta-study projects.

CRITERIA FOR EXCLUSION

The few researchers who have attempted a meta-synthesis of qualitative research have rather contradictory opinions about what exclusion criteria ought to be considered in determining the final sample of primary research reports (Sherwood, 1999). Jensen and Allen (1996), for example, argue that inclusion should not be restricted on the basis of the scientific merit of the research, as such judgments will eliminate data that might have been useful for the purposes of the meta-synthesis.

Our experience, however, has been that some kinds of inconsistencies and limitations in research reporting may jeopardize the perceived rigor of some of the available primary research. These include using unusual or skewed samples (especially when they are very small), omitting significant data or details of the research design, arriving at conclusions or categories that were not supported by the data provided in the report, analyzing research data that are congruent with a selected theoretical perspective while overlooking data that do not substantiate it, and failing to account for relevant data that are apparent to the reader in participants' quotes within the report (Field & Marck, 1994; Jensen & Allen, 1994, 1996).

Where the "political" agenda of a researcher is evident throughout the study, we have found it very difficult to accept the data on which the findings were based and the quality of the conclusions that were drawn. This kind of study, which Johnson (1999) has called "pseudoscience," or "uncritical verificationism," would be sufficiently questionable to make inclusion unwise if the integrity of the final meta-study product is to be maintained. Some researchers, for example, particularly in the early 1980s, used single interviews with very small samples of individuals (as few as one) as a basis for rather strong claims about findings that were representative of the entire experience of living with a chronic disease. In some cases, these reports were complicated by claims that the researcher had achieved theoretical saturation or redundancy (Sandelowski, 1995). Thus, in some instances, we did believe that the integrity of our meta-study would have been compromised if we had included certain types of primary research report.

In contrast with Jensen and Allen's (1996) opinion, Estabrooks and her colleagues (1994) recommend that all flawed research reports be omitted from a meta-synthesis sample. From our perspective, this view, too, presents difficulties. Among these is the reality that what might be considered flawed qualitative research at this point in time might have been considered quite acceptable 20 years ago. Another difficulty is that our interpretation of research quality is almost entirely grounded in our theoretical and methodological training, and so researchers of various disciplinary stripes will almost invariably favor the approaches that most closely resemble those integral to their own field. Yet another difficulty is one we learned from our own experience: What we as researchers regard as "flaws" are often reflections of our personal biases and quirks about the research process. Some of our most animated discussions as a research team arose when two or more people disagreed about the exclusion of a research report because of someone's perception that it was "flawed research."

All meta-study researchers must resolve this issue, however, and decide whether studies should be excluded if they are found to have design or reporting problems (Sherwood, 1999). Because the answer will be dependent on the nature of the meta-study, there is no easy formula to follow here. You will need to consider the purpose of the meta-study, the nature of your research question, the number of reports available to you, and the timeline of the research reports. Your decision will also depend on how you interpret each of these. For example, we discovered in the course of our project that the editorial policy of one highly respected journal routinely restricted what authors were permitted to write about the data analysis procedures of their research. Because of this policy, we concluded that the absence of detailed analytic processes should not be sufficient cause to exclude a research report from our meta-study as long as the author gave some indication of the general analytic strategy (e.g., constant comparative analysis) that was used.

We also learned that criteria for what counts as acceptable qualitative research have changed over time and will vary among different disciplines and researchers (Engel & Kuzel, 1992; Sandelowski et al., 1997; Silverman, 1998; Thorne, 1997). For example, we discovered that standards for qualitative research in nursing have focused primarily on methodological rigor at the expense of other quality measures such as theoretical integrity (Sandelowski et al., 1997). Educational researchers, however, have emphasized more than social scientists the utility and practical significance of the research findings (Wolcott, 1995). Thus, many of our original methodological assumptions were found to reflect disciplinary perspectives that might have systematically skewed our meta-study findings had we not rendered them as problematic and interpreted them. Of course, by including flawed research, the validity of the meta-study findings may be more difficult to defend in the final analysis (Cooper & Lindsay, 1998). However, we have been humbled by the fact that we rarely review qualitative research without some problematic aspects, including those reports written by ourselves.

Despite these issues, we have become convinced that a case can be made for articulating some methodological exclusion criteria beyond the matter of what constitutes a flaw. One instance in which the quality of data in primary research might be considered unacceptable for inclusion in a meta-study is when the depth and breadth of the data supplied by the author(s) are insufficient to convince the researcher that the findings are trustworthy. The comprehensiveness of research data in primary research reports can usually be determined by assessing (a) whether all data that are printed in the report, including participants' quotes, are accounted for in the research findings, (b) whether the data reported in the primary research are comprehensible, and (c) whether a clear relationship exists between the participants' responses and the categories of data reported by the author(s) of the primary research report (Hinds, Vogel, & Clarke-Steffen, 1997).

A variety of sources are available to assist you in determining the criteria to consider when evaluating the quality of primary research reports (e.g., Altheide & Johnson, 1994; Frankel, 1999; Lincoln, 1995; Sandelowski, 1993a; Sherwood, 1999; Thorne, 1997; Wolcott, 1990). In our chronic illness meta-study, decisions about the exclusion or inclusion of primary research on the basis of the trustworthiness of the findings were made according to the general standards for qualitative research proposed by Burns (1989) and adapted to fit the goals of meta-study. We encountered some primary research reports, for example, in which the researchers elaborated on concepts and frameworks well beyond the domain that the reported data or study findings appeared to permit. We reviewed other research reports in which the authors claimed to have used ethnography, phenomenology, or grounded theory but whose research designs were quite incongruent with the stated approach. Such studies were included or excluded from our meta-study on the basis of the degree to which they met Burns's standards of descriptive vividness, analytic preciseness, and heuristic relevance. Thus, in general, they would be included only if we could agree that the researchers had provided a clear description of how the research findings arose from the reported data.

One important insight we gained from our inaugural meta-study experience was the importance of keeping a complete record of all primary research reports that do not meet selection criteria and are subsequently excluded from the sample. Initially, we failed to appreciate the significance of this step and omitted it because it added a significant amount of labor to the project overall (we reviewed close to 1,000 research reports to extract the almost 300 we eventually included). As time passed, however, we found it difficult to recall the bases of decisions we had made to exclude a specific report when we later encountered a report with similar attributes. Had we retained a comprehensive record of such decisions, we would have been able to provide more detailed contextual information about what our meta-study included and what it did not, and why. This information would have assisted us in articulating more clearly the limitations and challenges associated with our selection criteria.

Because sampling decisions evolve in a meta-study project, the logic of inclusion and exclusion must always be explicit and consistent. Had we more meticulously recorded information about the road not traveled, we would have had access to a fascinating database for historical review of trends in qualitative health research over the past two decades. We might have discovered systematic privileging of the research products of certain disciplines, methods, or substantive themes as a result of our selection criteria. Thus, after our initial experience, we have included sufficient time and resources in our projects to ensure that this step will be adequately addressed. We are convinced that critical reflection on the implications of inclusion and exclusion decisions for the ultimate meta-study results will remain an important quality criterion in this kind of research.

APPRAISAL OF PRIMARY RESEARCH REPORTS

Once the challenge of retrieval is accomplished, it is equally essential to develop a systematic means for reviewing and appraising the theory, methods, and findings of selected research reports. Because this task must be done in a similar manner for all primary research reports, it is useful to develop a scheme at the onset of the meta-study project. We learned that the most expedient appraisal tool requires as little longhand as possible. By developing a form that could easily be distributed, completed, coded, and stored in computer databases (see Appendix A), we improved the effectiveness and efficiency of the review process and had an ongoing record of the findings for analysis. Our data collection instrument therefore became both a means to determine the report's eligibility for inclusion in the meta-study and a systematic way to record pertinent data about the primary research study.

Although meta-study is a team effort, we found it helpful to have one team member (usually the principal investigator) conduct a preliminary review of all reports and immediately exclude those that obviously did not meet our selection criteria in some clear and incontestable manner. On numerous occasions, however, we were able to determine whether a research report should be included only after a thorough assessment by several reviewers within our team. One study, for example, appeared to focus on the admission to hospital of persons with asthma in acute respiratory crisis. Despite our initial inclination to exclude the study because it dealt with an acute, not chronic, condition, having several team members complete the appraisal form and discuss this report helped us appreciate that the major findings actually revolved around important elements in the long-term aspects of coping with that particular health challenge.

Your decision whether to adapt an existing appraisal tool or to develop your own will depend on the criteria you recognize as most relevant to the goals of your particular research question. Thus, we encourage considerable discussion and deliberation before the final version is determined. We also suggest that you pilot-test your appraisal tool, using several research reports, before you make your final decision. The focus for such testing and refinement should not be whether it is possible to complete the tool, but rather whether the tool captures everything that will be important for future analysis. For example, we learned by trial and error that many of the questions in our original appraisal tool were not particularly relevant to our research question. Although we had originally adopted Burns's (1989) criterion relating to evidence of ethical approval, we came to realize that the degree to which this was reported was highly dependent on the journal, the discipline, and the historical period; at the same time, we recognized that the presence or absence of this information had no bearing on our ability to answer our own research question.

To determine the methodological congruence of each primary research report, we evaluated the sampling, data analysis, and data interpretation procedures according to rigor in documentation, rigor in procedure, and auditability (Burns, 1989). At least three team members reviewed every research report. If we did not arrive at a consensus about the assessment of the report, we met with additional team members to argue our viewpoints and come to a defensible decision. By requiring a consensus, we created a dialogical climate in which different opinions became the fodder for our evolving analysis of issues within the field and alerted us to subtleties within our own theoretical and perceptual leanings. Tracking such ideas as they evolve through the course of the research project produces excellent "field notes" for later use in deconstructing some of the ideas that come to seem self-evident once you have been immersed in the research reports over time. Finally, because the consensus decision reflected the one we wished to retain for further analysis, we had the data from the three (or more) original appraisal forms summarized into a single report by a research assistant and entered into our database.

In the interpretive paradigm of research, it is recognized that truths will be multiple and constructed; therefore, no two researchers will interpret research findings in quite the same way (Jensen & Allen, 1996; Miles, 1983). This presents a dilemma to meta-study researchers who may find it difficult to distinguish an alternative credible interpretation from a poorly conducted interpretive process (Angen, 2000). We sometimes arrived at quite different understandings from the data provided in primary research studies and those of the report's author(s). We then had to decide whether to consider the data as they were recorded or the conclusions about them to represent the central contribution of that particular study. If the latter, we preserved the words of the author(s) in recording the data categories. If the former, we considered changing the language with which the conclusions were articulated to fit better with the recorded data. Needless to say, any such decisions required deliberation about the impact of any variations from the original research report on the meta-study findings. Again, because the logic used in making such decisions must be explicit and auditable, careful recording of all such decisions is crucial.

In the actual application of the appraisal tool, the reviewers' responses to the criteria for appraising qualitative research reports are intended to be descriptive rather than evaluative. Thus, decisions made in the original research are not documented as right or wrong, appropriate or inappropriate. The nature of the sample in each research report illustrates why this is important. Among the studies we reviewed, typical samples were derived from nomination by health care professionals, taken from the register of physicians' or clinic clients, obtained by requesting volunteers from self-help organizations, or composed of self-selected volunteers. Although it is difficult to argue that one sampling technique is better or worse than any other (Conrad, 1990), each will influence the type of sample that is recruited and will lead to limitations in the generalizability of findings. In our diabetes meta-study project, for example, it became evident to us that many studies we reviewed obtained samples from diabetes support and education groups. We therefore had to ask ourselves how the nature of the sample would have influenced the findings accessible from the overall body of research and how the needs and experiences of those who choose to participate in such groups might be expected to differ from those of persons who choose not to participate.

We believe that several significant aspects of primary research reports should always be recorded as data by meta-study researchers. As the primary researcher is an instrument of qualitative research, it is important to appreciate and understand the influence of the researcher on the research design and the interpretation of the findings. Any available details about the lead investigator or primary author's disciplinary background, methodological preferences, and research collaborations may be revealing (Sandelowski et al., 1997). In some journals, the researcher's discipline is acknowledged within the body of the research report or as a footnote. In some instances, it can be extrapolated from the name of the department or research unit in which the researcher is employed or from the degrees indicated after the authors' names on the manuscript. Sometimes it is possible to make an educated guess at the disciplinary tradition of lead researchers by virtue of the particular theoretical perspectives or analytic frameworks that shape what and how they research certain phenomena and the way they interpret research findings. For example, researchers in both medicine and physiotherapy emphasize functional ability in their chronic illness research; this emphasis reveals how chronic illness knowledge has been constructed within those disciplines. Researchers in psychology more typically assume a behavioral or cognitive theoretical perspective. Researchers claiming to use a simultaneity paradigm or holistic theoretical approach would most likely reflect a nursing orientation.

In the course of our meta-study, we also discovered researchers whose work seemed more a representative of a specific school of thought than an investigation of the phenomenon of chronic illness. This inconsistency became problematic when the stated purpose of the research (i.e., to study the experience of living with a chronic illness) seemed secondary to validating a particular theoretical stance with which the researcher was aligned. For example, although the stated intention of one study was to investigate the experience of health within a specific chronic illness, the reported findings were limited to the ways in which the selected conceptual framework was accurate in describing this experience. In our chronic illness meta-study, we located five research studies whose apparent intent was to study ill persons for the purpose of validating a specific theory of illness. Such research relied heavily on the theoretical framework to phrase the questions posed in interviews, to categorize and conceptualize data, and to interpret results. Typically, competing interpretations of the phenomenon that might have been available in the literature were not considered. We therefore interpreted with considerable caution the findings of this category of research. Thus, beyond the disciplinary perspective, we found it essential to code and capture the theoretical frame and something about the way it influenced the research findings.

DEVELOPMENT OF A FILING AND CODING SYSTEM

At the onset of a meta-study project, it is wise to develop a method of filing the selected reports and of coding the results of the primary research appraisals so that the research team can quickly access these data. In our studies, we have concluded that it is preferable to file all data in two ways. Hard copies of the primary research reports and the completed appraisal forms are assigned numeric codes and are filed together in numeric order. Electronic copies of the appraisal forms are also stored in databases separate from the original research reports. Of course, it is essential that the numeric code for each study be readily accessible, and so accurate and up-to-date source lists (in full bibliographical style) are maintained both numerically and alphabetically.

Although we found that the hard copies were preferable for some of the reflection and interpretation activities, having an effective electronic record from which to work made many of our analytic processes considerably easier and more flexible. Each team member maintained an up-to-date reference list, which proved helpful both for cross-checking as we worked and for facilitating transfer of bibliographic content when it came time to writing reports. We also devised an electronic database that summarized many of the key variables related to each research report and that facilitated searching and sorting operations as our analytic questions became increasingly refined. This summary listed all primary reports numerically (by the number they were assigned) by year of publication, author(s), disease(s), major construct investigated, research approach, and "take-home message" (a concise summary of the research findings; see Appendix B). An electronic database such as this proved invaluable in helping us locate quickly those studies that dealt with specific constructs, chronic diseases, or sample sets and in highlighting trends and themes among the studies. Because the information that is eventually recorded and summarized in such a database may come to seem more relevant than data that are not so easily accessible to research team members, deciding what will be included and why should not be a matter of serious consideration.

ENSURING RIGOR

As with primary qualitative research, meta-study research must attend to the principles of rigor so that the research findings can be recognized as credible and trustworthy. In meta-study, these principles are largely addressed by attending to the appraisal of primary research reports and by documenting how and why decisions are made throughout the meta-study process. Researchers should determine the means to attain and maintain rigor at the onset of a meta-study project and institute these plans from the beginning. In our projects, we have used the following means to achieve trustworthiness (Lincoln & Guba, 1985):

- All reviews were conducted by three researchers independently.
- The reviewers met to identify differences in their reviews and to arrive at an agreement.
- Negative or disconfirming cases/incidents in the research were identified.
- Rival hypotheses were tested by seeking explanations other than the researchers' original hypothesis to describe the meta-study findings.

The rigor of a meta-study can be determined by four factors: (a) truth value, (b) applicability, (c) consistency, and (d) neutrality (Lincoln & Guba, 1985). The *truth value* of a meta-study lies in the faithfulness of the researcher in presenting data that resides in the primary research reports, rather than in the prior conceptions of the researcher (Sandelowski, 1986). A meta-study that has truth value is credible; that is, the data from primary research reports are presented in such a way that the authors of these reports would recognize the conclusions as compatible with their descriptions and interpretations of the phenomenon under study. *Applicability* refers to the consistency between the meta-study conclusions and the domains within which the interpretations may have impact. In most instances, this criterion would reflect the clinical phenomenon toward which the study was directed, and the arbiters of applicability would be those most intimately connected to the field (Sandelowski, 1986). *Consistency* relates to the degree to which the conclusions follow logically from the research processes and analytic steps. It is typically determined by the auditability of a study or the degree to which the reader can follow the decision trail. It requires that meta-study researchers clearly identify and make explicit their decisions regarding research design and the interpretation of findings. Finally, *neutrality* refers to the freedom from bias in the process and outcome of the meta-study. These four criteria can be achieved in the following ways in meta-study research:

- Describe and explain the rationale for what you did throughout the meta-study research process. This means being as clear as possible about the purpose of the meta-study, the sampling of primary research reports, the theoretical framework chosen, the data collection, and the data interpretation. Avoid using labels or academic jargon, as these often mean different things to different readers and your intent may not always be clear (Sandelowski, 1986).

- Document the procedures you used and the decisions you made throughout the processes of meta-study. This will permit other researchers to determine the trustworthiness of the study.

- Maintain and have available the theoretical and methodological memos you wrote throughout the meta-study process. Also, maintain a record of the way data were coded and any schematic representations of relationships among data. Methodological notes include the insights, questions, and difficulties you encounter throughout the research processes. Theoretical notes include your thinking about the data derived from the meta-study processes. For example, members of our team made notations about the possible sociocultural influences of the primary research and raised questions about how the data from one primary research report might connect to others they had read.

- Check your meta-study findings against those of the primary research reports to determine that your meta-study includes both typical and atypical elements of the theory, interpretations, and descriptions of the phenomena located in the primary research (Sandelowski, 1986).

- Attempt to discount or discredit your interpretations of the data by continually asking questions about the meta-study data (Sandelowski, 1986).

- Check the origins of data by placing the location of the data beside their codes. For example, as codes were entered into the computer, we identified the source(s) from which they were derived (e.g., "economic costs = #6 pp. 35-37, #15, #39 summary").

- Meet as a research team on a regular basis to discuss methodological and theoretical issues that arise in the course of the meta-study. Minutes of these meetings should provide a detailed account of how the team made decisions regarding these issues.

- Meta-study findings should be "cautiously applied and critically interpreted" (Aldag & Stearns, 1998, p. 261). To minimize the risk of making overly broad generalizations, qualify the conclusions of your meta-study with information about the kinds of qualitative methods/people/disease conditions included, those that were not included, and those that were overrepresented (Cooper & Lindsay, 1998). For example, in articles we write about aspects of our chronic illness meta-study, we include statements that most participants in the primary research have been well-educated, middle-class, Caucasian women. We note that certain diseases receive disproportionate attention in the research, whereas others are relatively unstudied. We caution readers that this disproportion significantly limits the applicability of findings from the available research to the general chronic illness population.

From our experience using this method, we offer a caution about the pursuit of rigor in meta-study research. There is often so much data to share in reports emanating from the meta-study that it is tempting to sacrifice the richness of description for precision (Aldag & Stearns, 1998). Conducting a meta-study involves a delicate juggling of creativity and magic (May, 1994) with rigor and precision. In an effort to provide a clear trail indicating how we selected and analyzed data, we initially emphasized rigor and precision and did not allow for our imaginations to open new possibilities within the process. This emphasis turned out to make the process dry and tedious, but we also found that our conceptualizations of what was uncovered in the data were limited and not particularly revealing. Consequently, we began to institute research team meetings in which we often engaged in creative brainstorming of thoughts that occurred to us about the primary research we had reviewed to date. These thoughts were as diverse as comments about how the shape of specific research methods had changed over the years, queries about the relationship between two seemingly unrelated concepts, and suggestions about improving our review process. Often, our ideas and thoughts were loose and "half baked" in the early stages of wrestling with them. In our research team meetings, we capitalized on the diversity of perspectives within the group to argue them out and see whether they might hold up under challenge. These discussions were often the impetus for new insights about possible analytic angles by which to interpret the research data or new ways to approach the process of synthesis and fostered our continued excitement about the meta-study.

CONCLUSION

We have identified some of the challenges that confront meta-study researchers as they select primary research reports to include in their meta-study projects. We do not pretend that our list of challenges in this regard is exhaustive; many more will come to light as the research approach of meta-study is used by nursing and health care researchers other than ourselves. Each new meta-study project may well produce unique and different challenges, as well as insights about the access and selection of primary research. Although the challenges may initially seem daunting, they are readily addressed by clear and logical decisions about why and how specific primary research will be included or excluded. Although guidelines and principles are essential, the inductive processes required of this research absolutely demand the ability to extend analysis beyond the boundaries of the most obvious and acceptable interpretations.

4

META-DATA-ANALYSIS

Meta-data-analysis is the analysis of "processed data" from selected qualitative research studies to create a systematically developed, integrated body of knowledge about a specific phenomenon (Zhao, 1991). In meta-data-analysis, analysis of data takes place by comparing each individual report with all other reports that have a common focus or that share specific and generic properties (e.g., all research relating to the experience of living with arthritis). In addition, it permits the data of each individual study to be reexamined in the interpretive light of the conclusions that were derived from other studies in the field. Meta-data-analysis is not a single technique but rather "a flexible set of techniques" (Cook & Leviton, 1980, p. 469) that can be adapted to the research question and to the information provided in primary research reports. We have interpreted meta-data-analysis to mean the comparative analysis of research findings of primary research studies conducted by a variety of researchers.

Although many reports available in the literature refer to themselves as meta-synthesis, we discuss them here (rather than in Chapter 7) because they most closely resemble the comparative techniques and analytic operations of meta-data-analysis than the synthesis of new interpretations based on thorough critical reflection about the field of research. Examples of this kind of research are Statham et al.'s (1988) work on research on women's work; Morse and Johnson's (1991) and Jensen and Allen's (1994) syntheses of qualitative studies about illness; Field and Marck's (1994) synthesis of uncertain motherhood; Penrod and Morse's (1997) development of a theory of uncertainty from qualitative studies that examined the illness experience; Sherwood's (1997) synthesis of qualitative research on caring in nursing; Burke, Kaufmann, Costello, Wiskin, and Harrison's (1998) analysis of stressors in families with chronically ill children; Kearney's (1998) theory development in the area of women's addiction recovery; and Barroso and Powell-Cope's (2000) study of the experience of adults living with HIV infection. Perhaps the most well known meta-data-analysis is by Noblit and Hare (1988), who conducted a meta-ethnography of qualitative research in education. Each of these has contributed to our understanding of how competing and isolated perspectives are connected and interrelated in the phenomenon under study (Dluhy, 1995).

THE PURPOSE

Meta-data-analysis contributes to the overall aim of meta-study—that is, to extend knowledge about a particular phenomenon in a field of study (Schreiber et al., 1997; Sherwood, 1999). This is most relevant when a multitude of perspectives about a particular phenomenon exist and appear to be disconnected and at times dichotomous (Dluhy, 1995). The body of knowledge that emanates from such competing perspectives is often inexplicable to the practicing clinician who must attempt to decipher what is relevant to apply to the care of clients. In our chronic illness meta-study, we discovered that several researchers proposed that living with a chronic illness may enable individuals to experience life, themselves, and others in a way that was inaccessible before their conditions were diagnosed; that is, they may be transformed. Transformation is not described beyond generalities by many researchers, and what has been described is not particularly revealing. Thus, it is not clear from this body of research why some people experience transformation and others do not. Using meta-data-analysis, we were able to identify the structure and processes of transformation in chronic illness. We were also able to describe whether, how, and why transformation occurs (Paterson, Thorne, Crawford, & Tarko, 1999). Perhaps most significant, we were able to determine how clinicians might most appropriately apply what we had learned in the care of clients with chronic illness.

Meta-data-analysis can be used to test and validate substantive theory arising from primary research (Steeves et al., 1996). In our research, for example, we posed some questions of the text of the primary research studies in the chronic illness meta-study to determine whether the theory of uncertainty was supported by the text. We discovered contradictions to the current interpretation of the theory, including that persons with chronic illness may respond to uncertainty as a challenge, not as a source of fear. In meeting that challenge, persons with chronic illness may experience a transformation in the way they view and derive meaning from the experience of living with a chronic illness.

DATA IN META-DATA-ANALYSIS

Before we describe the actual procedures of meta-data-analysis, it is important to understand what is meant by the term *data* in this context. The data in meta-data-analysis are obtained from the text of primary research reports. Text may be one or two words or a sentence or a paragraph. Claims of what primary researchers have revealed as findings are subject to the meta-study researcher's personal filter. Consequently, what is identified as meaningful data by meta-study researchers is influenced by their views of what seems credible within the interpretations. No matter what approach you use for meta-data-analysis, you must read the report thoroughly and then decide what textual elements, or units of data, are in the research findings of that report, whether depicted as themes, categories, domains, patterns, or processes.

You should be able to retain the meaning of the text once it is removed from the context of the report. It is rarely sufficient to copy down words or phrases of codes or categories used by the authors of primary research reports as data for the meta-data-analysis. You cannot expect to recall the full meaning of those terms when you review the appraisal tool concerning that research several days or weeks later. For example, Paterson and Sloan (1994) originally identified a major category of their findings as "collaboration with health care professionals" (p. 17). Later, in consultation with the meta-study research team, Paterson was no longer convinced that this phrase effectively captured the intended meaning of the category as it was depicted in the original research. The meta-study team made the intent more explicit by rephrasing that finding in the appraisal as "expert decision makers in Type I diabetes select and teach health care professionals to be partners with them in decisions about the disease management."

Text in meta-data-analysis is not as straightforward as we had initially imagined. At the onset of our chronic illness meta-study, we believed analyzing text to be a relatively simple process of recording and sorting the categories and themes identified by the authors. We soon discovered that the categories/themes explicated by researchers are not always supported by the data they report. As well, sometimes the category/theme chosen by a researcher does not sufficiently capture the data that are provided (as was the case in the above example). This meant that the reviewers had to read and reread the report to ensure that the textual elements were accurate and supported by data within the report. At times, this rereading resulted in a decision to exclude the research report from the meta-study.

The following is an example of how data were derived from the text of a primary research report in our chronic illness meta-study. Loomis and Conco (1991) investigated the perceptions of 19 persons who received home care for a chronic illness. One major category of data identified by the primary researchers was "experiences of health and illness." The members of our team who reviewed this primary research report thought that such a category did not reveal the rich data the primary researchers used to support the category. They clarified the category by developing subcategories derived from a synopsis of the primary researchers' description of the category and quotes made by study participants. Subsequently, the category was represented in the following manner in our appraisal tool:

Experiences of Health and Illness:

- Health is the ability to do for self and to approximate normal functioning.

- Illness is the presence of physical symptoms that disturb the person's ability to function as she or he would like.

- Illness is described in terms of previous status ("Not half as bad as I used to be") and the larger picture ("Chronic illness is not a disease").

- None of the participants expected a cure, but all wanted to gain control of those things that limited their functioning.

- Positive attitude, medications that diminish disturbing symptoms, and accepting one's limitations lead to health.

Thus, the data on which meta-data-analysis is based are themselves open for interpretation, and interpretive steps must be carefully managed and documented from the outset of the project.

SELECTION OF ANALYTIC APPROACH

Meta-data-analysis consists of (a) the study of the underlying assumptions of various data analysis procedures, (b) the comparison of different forms of data in terms of their quality and utility, and (c) the synthesis of research findings of various studies in a particular area of research (Cooper, 1984). The first step in this process is to select a data analytic approach.

Data analysis techniques and procedures that are typical in primary research are also applicable to meta-data-analysis in meta-study. We believe that any systematic interpretive approach used in the analysis of data in a single study can be applicable to meta-data-analysis in a meta-study. Meta-study researchers choose a data analysis strategy that fits with their research question and design, as well as the prevailing paradigm and their personal preference. Researchers who are investigating a process-oriented construct (e.g., decision-making) may choose to conduct meta-data-analysis in accordance with the grounded theory approach to data analysis (Glaser & Strauss, 1967; Strauss & Corbin, 1990). Other approaches to meta-data-analysis are meta-ethnography (Noblit & Hare, 1988), thematic analysis (Morse, 1997; Morse & Johnson, 1991; Penrod & Morse, 1997), and interpretive descriptive analysis (Thorne, Kirkham, & MacDonald-Emes, 1997).

Although several analytic methods are appropriate in meta-data-analysis, some unique features of meta-study prohibit strict adherence to some of the available techniques. To illustrate, although the constant comparative method of data analysis first described by Glaser and Strauss (1967) is a systematic and efficient means of analyzing data derived from primary research reports, it depends on an ongoing generation of new data and sampling until all categories of data are saturated. In meta-study, the saturation of categories may not occur because of the restrictions inherent in the primary data set. For example, we located only five research studies that specifically explored the impact of technological devices, such as ventilators, on living with a chronic illness. Several hypotheses arose from the data of these studies (e.g., persons who can receive immediate feedback about their physiological status are able to make self-care decisions more readily than those without such feedback), but they could not be fully examined because the data to support or negate these hypotheses were insufficient. As shown in this instance, the inability to saturate categories of data may result in a limited emerging theory (Szabo & Strang, 1997).

The analytic approach that is chosen in meta-data-analysis will determine the procedures employed for data analysis. If you have chosen to conduct data analysis in accordance with grounded theory as described by Strauss and Corbin (1990), for example, you would identify text units in the findings of each research report and then code them by using in vivo and metaphorical codes, making explicit the defining characteristics and the dimensions of these codes. Noblit and Hare (1988) give a step-by-step description of meta-ethnography, a meta-data-analysis approach in the ethnographic tradition. We used this approach in our chronic illness meta-study and found it particularly helpful in revealing similarities, differences, and lines of argument among the selected research reports.

THE META-STUDY APPROACH TO META-DATA-ANALYSIS

Regardless of the explicit analytic approach selected, meta-data-analysis involves two discrete aspects: hermeneutic and dialectic (Jensen & Allen, 1996). *Hermeneutic processes* in meta-data-analysis involve depicting accurate representations of the individual constructions (Baszanger & Dodier, 1998; Reeder, 1988). *Dialectic processes* entail comparing the intentions of the author of those constructions with the interpretations rendered accessible to the reader (Crotty, 1998). As we discussed in Chapter 3, our approach to meta-data-analysis differs from that advocated by some proponents of meta-synthesis in relation to such strategies as the selection of primary research reports (particularly with reference to homogeneity of research methods and inclusion of all research reports regardless of scientific merit).

Another major difference between our approach and those of others is that we advocate a multifaceted rather than singular grouping system to analyze primary research data. An example is Jensen and Allen's (1994) meta-ethnography of qualitative research concerning health, disease, wellness, and illness, the goal of which was to develop a model of wellness-illness. In that study, data were analyzed according to the articulated purpose of primary studies using the same qualitative research method. Similarly, Estabrooks and her colleagues (1994) used a method they termed "aggregating findings" to develop midrange theory through grouped findings in a qualitative meta-analysis. In our research, we strategically grouped the data from primary research reports in several ways, including by disease, by nature of the sample (e.g., gender, ethnicity, method of sampling), by whether the disease was considered terminal or not, by decade of publication, and by research method. The data representing the experience of a specific group of participants or the experience of living with a particular chronic illness were analyzed separately, as a unique case, and then integrated with all research reports as a whole. The advantages of treating each grouping as a case, compared with compiling the data from all chronic illness research and analyzing them as a whole, is that similarities and differences, as well as outliers and negative and extreme cases, are more readily identified.

As an example, in the chronic illness meta-study, we analyzed all data relating to the experience of living with Type I diabetes and then compared them with the data regarding the experience of living with Type II diabetes. Then we compared them with the data arising from all chronic illness research reports included in the meta-study. We discovered that an essential difference in the experience of Type I and Type II diabetes is the perception of risk. In Type I diabetes, the perception of risk of hypoglycemia in self-care management is generally considerably higher than in Type II, and this influences the nature of the self-care decisions a person with Type I diabetes makes. We also noted that individuals with diabetes differ in their responses to diabetes and in their perceptions of the ability to control the impact of the disease in comparison with individuals who have other chronic diseases. The difference was most apparent in the data regarding Type I diabetes and pertained to both the use of glucometers for immediate feedback about glycemic status and the efficacy of decisions that had been made. This finding was significant in our determining the potential impact of a technological measuring device on the nature of self-care decision making in chronic illness.

Perhaps the most significant difference between our approach to meta-data-analysis and those of other meta-synthesists is our emphasis on the contextual nature of primary research data. Data are shaped methodologically and theoretically by the researcher's theoretical orientation and research design and historically and socioculturally by what was happening at the time of the research. In our meta-data-analysis of 43 research reports that appeared to cover 38 discrete studies of the experience of living with diabetes (Paterson, Thorne, & Dewis, 1998), we not only analyzed the data from these studies but also examined them in the light of the context of the primary research. We noted that the primary research reflected the researchers' allegiance to theories of client empowerment and self-care, the rising awareness among the public of clients' rights, and the predominance of singular, retrospective interviews with Caucasian, well-educated participants. From this analysis, we concluded that the context of the research had contributed to the emphasis within these studies on both active participation and compliance in diabetes management.

DATA MANAGEMENT

Data analysis and data management are closely intertwined. We discussed some aspects of data management in Chapter 3. However, some unique aspects of data management are specific to meta-data-analysis. You will need to make projections about the format of data records for the meta-data-analysis before the meta-study begins. Much of this work depends on the nature of the data that will be pertinent to the research question. In our chronic illness meta-study, for example, we were aware that we would want to compare and contrast the experience of those of diverse ethnicity, and therefore we included a section for reviewers to indicate the ethnicity of the sample.

Records of all coding structures in the meta-data-analysis should be maintained, including initial codes, decisions to collapse codes and categories, and sources in the primary research where the data are located. Such a record provides an audit trail of data analysis decisions and assists researchers who might wish to replicate or extend the inquiry (Rodgers & Cowles, 1993). Our coding system evolved throughout the meta-study as we refined and expanded our initial projections of the data we would need. Toward the conclusion of our chronic illness meta-study, for example, we recognized that we ought to record the researcher's relationship to the participants apart from the research study. This insight arose when we encountered a few primary research studies in which the researcher was also the health care professional from whom the participants received their health care. Not surprisingly, this group of researchers tended to conclude that their participants were positive about their relationships with their professional caregivers. Similarly, not until we began to isolate a category relating to the meaning of work for persons with chronic illness did we realize that we needed to record when participants of various primary research studies had a change in employment status following diagnosis of their illness. In keeping with the inductive nature of the analytic process, this realization led us to recognize the invisibility of any explicit consideration of worklife issues in many of the primary research reports.

We originally intended to use the NUD*IST software program (Richards & Richards, 1994) to analyze our research findings; however, we soon discovered that the decision-tree feature of this program was too linear and hierarchical to represent effectively the complex and multidimensional relationships of specific constructs within the experience of chronic illness. The NUD*IST program was helpful in determining the frequency of certain findings, and we were able to use its indexing and searching features to ask questions such as, "How many studies included non-Caucasian participants, and of these, how many referred to chronic illness as a loss or a burden?"

We maintained several records of the data analysis structures. Our coding structures (categories, subcategories, codes) were recorded by using NUD*IST computer software's decision-tree feature. We kept in a filing cabinet the hard copies of the coding scheme and the thesaurus of various codes. We also recorded explanations and descriptions of the codes and categories by using a word processing program. Finally, we wrote abstract summaries or the "take home message" for each primary research report and included these tabular forms along with other salient features of the primary research report (e.g., see Appendix B). Such summaries were helpful in permitting quick reviews of what was found in the primary research, as well as a further test of our analytic honesty. If our data analysis did not capture the essence of what the primary researcher thought the study was about, for example, we knew we had to revisit our interpretations.

ONE ANALYTIC APPROACH

We found Noblit and Hare's (1988) approach to meta-ethnography particularly useful in the meta-data-analysis phase of our large meta-study project. Noblit and Hare define meta-ethnography of qualitative research as "a study in itself" (p. 9). Unlike meta-analysis of quantitative research (Cooper & Linsday, 1998), meta-ethnography is interpretative, requiring the researcher to compare and analyze texts and reports of primary research findings, creating new interpretations in the process. This analytic process includes the development of hypotheses as the research progresses and the testing of these hypothetical relationships by means of further data collection and analysis in the search for confirming or disconfirming evidence to support or negate the emerging theory (Hutchinson, 1986; Stern & Pyles, 1986).

In meta-ethnography, each primary study is translated into metaphors that are then compared with the metaphors of others to generate a new interpretation that encompasses all reports (Jensen & Allen, 1996). This process adopts the interpretive frame of each study and examines how it might have been applied to all others in the set. In this way, it involves a continuous comparative analysis of the texts until a comprehensive understanding of the phenomenon is realized. The steps for this process are as follows:

1. Read each primary research report in detail, noting how the phenomenon is described. Pretend this is a transcript of an interview, and make notes about the concepts, key metaphors, categories, and phrases that best describe the phenomenon.

2. Compare and contrast the data in this primary research report with the data in other studies, as a whole or in subgroups, noting the similarities and differences between the key metaphors for each study. The most challenging aspect of a meta-data-analysis is developing strategies to compare and contrast primary research studies (Sandelowski et al., 1997).

We used various techniques to conduct such a comparison. One such strategy included the development of a coding schedule, entered into the NUD*IST software program, so that relationships between major categories of data could be recorded in a decision tree. Another involved visual data displays or drawing schematic representations of the relationships among codes, key metaphors, concepts, and ideas about the experience under study (Miles & Huberman, 1994).

3. Hypothesize about the nature of the relationships between studies (e.g., Do all the studies that mention visibility of chronic illness also refer indirectly or directly to stigma?) and, if possible, depict these relationships in a schematic representation.

4. Translate the primary research studies into one another by determining how the key metaphors of each study relate to those of other accounts, refining these translations until the phenomenon is described in a way that is faithful to the interpretations of the original data; that is, it accurately portrays the shared and unique findings of the included research studies.

Using our diabetes project, we illustrate here how we applied these meta-ethnography procedures to our meta-data-analysis. We read and reviewed 43 primary research reports of the experience of living with diabetes. In each of these, we identified specific themes and metaphors. We recognized that the participants of the various studies expressed many of these themes (e.g., "being controlled by the disease," "the disease controlling you") as if they were in dynamic tension to one another; the concept of balance emerged as the predominant determining metaphor of the experience of living with diabetes. As a means of testing this as a central category of data, we developed a table (see Paterson et al., 1998) to identify the various ways in which the balance metaphors were expressed and the primary sources from which these arose. This strategy assisted us in discovering that the metaphor of balance was credible because it was so well represented in each of the 43 reports. The interpretation of balance varied among studies, particularly in research involving participants of certain demographic characteristics. For example, we discovered that research participants who were mothers were more likely than other participants to perceive managing their diabetes as a lower priority than maintaining the well-being of their families. *Balance* for the participants of these primary studies was termed "the need for metabolic control" rather than "the needs of family and friends."

A crucial task in meta-data-analysis is developing a table to indicate the specific constructs that were studied by primary researchers in the meta-study and comparing this with a table of relevant concepts in the field. In the chronic illness meta-study, for example, we reviewed the literature about the experience of chronic illness and identified all salient constructs and concepts (e.g., fatigue, stress, specific diseases) in that body of literature. We then compared this with the list of concepts investigated in the primary research studies included in the meta-study. We found that the majority of those studies related to the experience of living with diabetes (44 of the 292 reports), cancer (41), and HIV/AIDS (26). Few studies pertained to such diseases as Parkinson's disease (3) or end-stage renal disease (6). We then had to ask the question, "Why were these diseases omitted in the study of chronic illness?" We brainstormed possible reasons (e.g., funding for research relating to certain diseases is greater than for others; some disease experiences are more popular to study than others). These reasons in turn led us to speculate about further rationale (e.g., Is AIDS more popular than COPD as a research topic because of the age of clients and the perceived tragedy of the illness?) and to return to the literature for further evidence to support or negate the suppositions we had raised.

Through this process, we gained relevant insights about the field. We learned that no qualitative research related to HIV/AIDS or the environmental diseases (e.g., fibromyalgia) had been conducted until the early 1990s. In contrast, we learned that the popularity of epilepsy as a focus of study disappeared after the 1980s. We found that, although disability and chronic illness were often considered in the same studies in the 1980s, disability achieved its own distinct cadre of researchers in the 1990s. We also discovered that, according to the perspective of many researchers, chronic illness was a rather generic phenomenon and that findings related to one disease (e.g., diabetes) were assumed to apply to others (e.g., multiple sclerosis). Finally, we learned that research conducted in the 1980s focused primarily on loss, dysfunction, attributions about the cause, assuming the sick role, uncertainty, suffering, change, coping, and negative societal and family attitudes, whereas research in the 1990s centered on self-management of the disease, health within illness, the trajectory of learning to assume control, meaning, hope, courage, sexuality, quality of life, transcendence, challenge, discovery, and mastery (Thorne & Paterson, 1998).

The exercise of tabling the nature and findings of the primary research studies also revealed the differences in researchers' interpretations of the phenomenon under study. In our chronic illness meta-study, for example, those researchers who investigated the experience of living with a disease with potential for rehabilitation (e.g., myocardial infarction, first-stage cancer) often reported more hope for the future and a greater sense of personal control than did those who studied the experience of living with a disease with a degenerative or terminal prognosis. We were left with several questions to explore: Do researchers investigate diseases with expectations of hope/hopelessness or control/powerlessness? Is this reflected in their research design? How does the prognosis of a disease affect the experience of hope and control of those with the disease?

The procedures by Noblit and Hare (1988) allowed for the creativity and flexibility that is inherent in qualitative research while, at the same time, providing structure for the meta-data-analysis. Accordingly, we developed hypotheses as the research progressed and tested these hypothetical relationships by means of further data collection—that is, by reading and extracting data from the selected reports. Estabrooks and colleagues (1994) are critical of this approach, stating that it is context stripping and does not focus on the generation of midrange theory. As we have illustrated, we were able to consider context within the procedures of meta-ethnography. Noblit and Hare state that context is essential in the analysis of research findings among selected reports, including historical and cultural contexts. Explorations of the shifting trends such as those we have identified in our studies clearly demand such contextual analysis.

Although meta-ethnography procedures are relatively straightforward in substance and application, particularly if the meta-study researcher has previous experience with this approach to data analysis, we encourage you to explore other methods of data analysis that might be more appropriate to the research question(s), intended audience, and desired outcomes of your own meta-data-analysis. For example, you may wish a less structured approach that permits you to develop analytic categories through a creative inductive approach, such as the interpretive descriptive method described by Thorne and her colleagues (1997). Penrod and Morse (1997) describe an alternate data-analysis process in which the primary research findings must be "unraveled" so that researchers immerse themselves in the main themes and messages of the data, rather than confine their insights to the formulation of codes and categories.

REMAINING ANALYTICALLY HONEST

One danger in meta-data-analysis is that meta-study researchers will select codes or categories that are more in keeping with their interpretation of the phenomenon under study than those the primary researcher may have intended. Meta-study researchers may also tend to place too much weight on limited data because the data support what they believe to be true. They may ignore data that do not support their reasoning. They may select data that confirm their ideas more often than data that contradict them (Miles & Huberman, 1994). To avoid such temptations, you must keep "analytically honest" (Miles & Huberman, 1994, p. 253). Here are some strategies to help you in this aspect of your work:

- Conduct the data analysis in groups of at least three. In our chronic illness meta-study, each primary research report was analyzed by three team members independently. Effective colleagues often present ideas that reveal different interpretations of what the data represent. Such challenges cause you to defend your analysis, revealing both the strengths and the limitations of your analytic processes.

- Include as much direct information as possible from the report on the appraisal tool in regard to the codes or categories you have developed. This inclusion will enable your team members to revisit the analysis and to determine whether support for the codes and categories that have been identified is adequate.

- Develop a table in which you identify the major categories and the sources from which they were derived. This overview of the data sources will assist you in identifying when you have overemphasized aspects of the data, giving it more importance than the occasional representation in the primary research has warranted.

- Avoid rapid categorizing of overarching categories or predominant metaphors. Such categorization can become a self-fulfilling prophecy, and you may find that you "see into" the data to find evidence that supports your categorization. Miles and Huberman (1994) suggest waiting until at least two thirds of the data analysis is completed before you attempt categorization and then going back over the collected data to test it.

- Reflect on the metaphors you choose to code or categorize the data. They often reveal the underlying assumptions you hold about the phenomenon under study. In our chronic illness meta-study, we often coded data as "control." A discussion among the research team revealed that this term had varied meanings for each of us (e.g., compliance, independence, ability to overcome symptoms) and that each meaning had implications for how we interpreted the data.

- Be aware of categories or codes that appear "too tidy" and that appear to capture all variations and contradictions in the data. Categories that account for all data may be too broad to be meaningful. Alternatively, you may find that you have ignored significant data because they do not fit neatly into the category you have selected.

CONCLUSION

Meta-data-analysis is a systematic means of combining the findings of several qualitative research studies concerning a specific phenomenon. Such a process relegates qualitative research studies from isolated islands of information to an integrated body of knowledge about a particular phenomenon under study (Sandelowski et al., 1997). It requires the meta-study researcher to be skilled in the translation of semantic, literal, or idiomatic meaning within the text of primary research reports (Noblit & Hare, 1988). Our experiences with meta-data-analysis have convinced us that by using a rigorous, transparent, and reflexive analytic process, it creates the conditions under which the common insights discernible from a body of qualitative research studies can be rendered visible, analyzed, and interpreted. Similarly, our experiences teach us that meta-data-analysis is but one part of a thorough and rigorous meta-analytic process.

5

META-METHOD

M*eta-method* is the study of the epistemological soundness of the existing research, as well as the ways the methodological applications may have influenced the findings that are generated. Meta-method includes (a) examination of "methodological presuppositions necessary for carrying out" the research (Zhao, 1991, p. 378), (b) evaluation of the research methods in terms of weaknesses and limitations, and (c) codification of new procedural norms for research in the area (Richman, 1983). An excellent example of meta-method is the article by Charmaz and Olesen (1997) in which they review ethnographic research in medical sociology to demonstrate how this research method has "changed the picture of illness" (p. 57) over time. Although the two authors did not refer to the review as meta-method, it is in keeping with the tenets of meta-method because they concluded with detailed new directives for researchers in the area of study.

THE PURPOSE

The purpose of meta-method is to determine how the interpretation and implementation of qualitative research methods have influenced the research findings and the emergent theory in a particular field of knowledge.

71

Although this requires an appraisal of primary research reports, the intent of appraisal is not to critique the quality of the individual studies, but rather to consider how the methodology that has been applied to the study of a phenomenon has shaped current understandings about it. Meta-method also permits several secondary purposes. It can assist the researcher in conducting a historical review of research methods within a particular discipline or within a specific field of research. From such a foundation, it is possible to develop new insights about the implications of how various methodological strategies shape knowledge and to propose strategies for ways research methods may be more appropriately applied to knowledge development in the field. Within a meta-study, the meta-method process creates an opportunity to reflect critically on how qualitative research methods have been applied during a specified period of time and in relation to a specific question or issue. This analysis provides valuable insights for nursing research by revealing "what factors in the world of research, in general, and in nursing research, in particular, frame the intellectual processes of disciplined curiosity, reasoned inquiry, and painstaking experimentation" (D'Antonio, 1997, p. 105).

Using the procedures of meta-method, the meta-study researcher can examine how the use of these methods has changed over time and can document the impact of these changes on how researchers have designed their research and ultimately on the findings they achieve. An example is Gerhardt's (1990) review of how qualitative research methods in the field of chronic illness have changed or become more or less popular with researchers, depending on the sociocultural and political influences of the time. While conducting meta-method analysis for our chronic illness meta-study, we noticed the popularity of ethnographic methods and also its evolution as various researchers adapted traditional approaches in response to the specific participants, context, and illness experiences they were studying. For example, Gregory (1994) rejected the intense and prolonged interaction with research participants usually required in ethnographic studies in order to accommodate the pain, fatigue, and social distance experienced by his research participants with terminal cancer.

Similarly, we noticed trends in the application of grounded theory methodology in chronic illness experience research to distance it from its traditional association with symbolic interactionism and to consider both intrapsychic and subjective embodied processes along with those that are more inherently social. Whereas an earlier era of critics might have considered such applications to be "method slurring" (Baker, Wuest, & Stern, 1992), we have been able to appreciate how creatively researchers have applied their chosen method so that they can capture the nuances and unique attributes of the phenomenon under study in a manner more epistemologically sound than would be knowledge gleaned from a more purist approach (Lawler, 1998; Thorne et al., 1997).

Meta-method also permits an alternative interpretation of how fundamental disciplinary assumptions shape the research we do and the conclusions we come to on the basis of that research. We have been struck, for example, by the way certain methodological variations become popular within a discipline or a particular national community of researchers and how, over time, the reference points for interpreting the total body of knowledge can become more insular. As the body of qualitative research directed toward a particular phenomenon expands, it can become increasingly tempting to narrow one's focus and to acknowledge only a small portion of the available knowledge in justifying the methodological approach to a new study. Because we have understood the study of chronic illness experience, for example, to be inherently interdisciplinary, we were somewhat startled to read recent research reports that locate a research question entirely within one methodological or disciplinary tradition. Thus, we have seen the field of chronic illness research move from a rather narrow beginning, in which most research was sociological in focus, toward a broader and more interdisciplinary phase, and back again into discrete disciplinary silos.

Through meta-method procedures, we have discovered a great deal about ourselves as researchers and have been challenged to reflect on the ways our own methodological preferences may have shaped what we consider legitimate and useful knowledge about chronic illness experience. As was suggested by Szmatka and Lovaglia (1996), we recognize that research methods have significantly influenced the theory that has developed from research. For example, as Silverman (1998) points out, we know far more about chronic illness experience from research methods that use open-ended interviews as a data collection strategy than we know from participant observation or conversational analysis. Thus, the analysis of method as a critically important feature in its own right contributes a different species of insights and interpretations to a metastudy project.

THE PROCEDURE

The procedure of meta-method involves comparing and contrasting the research designs of primary research reports to identify underlying assumptions and trends in the understanding of research methodologies, as well as the outcomes (data or theory) associated with specific research methods. It entails two steps: (a) the initial appraisal of individual primary research studies regarding research design and data collection, and (b) an overall appraisal of the themes and patterns evident within the collection of primary research studies included in the meta-study.

As in all other components of meta-study, meta-method is an interpretive process, subject to the interpretations of the meta-study researchers. In many instances, interpretation will be enhanced by an intimate familiarity with the subtleties and nuances within the methodological claims of the primary research. Because there is no universal language by which research methods are described (Ray, 1994), language usage is an obvious target for interpretation. For example, although a researcher may claim a phenomenological approach to a particular inquiry, use of the language deriving from symbolic interactionism or a focus on basic social processes may alert the meta-method analyst to the probable influence of grounded theory methodology. Other reference points are the methodological citations used by a researcher to locate various methodological options. Even though traditional wisdom might lead you to assume that ethnographers would usually cite ethnographic methods as sources to support their decisions about entry into the field, identification of participants, data analysis, and so on, we have been surprised by the degree to which qualitative health researchers draw on a range of methodologically distinct sources for their procedural guidance. Clearly, detecting apparent inconsistencies and incongruities in methodological application will be considerably more difficult for the neophyte researcher or for the researcher with limited appreciation for the linguistic and reference cues by which methodological options are described.

Although focused attention on methodological curiosities typically reveals all sorts of insights about how different researchers have approached their research questions, it is also important that the meta- method analyst not jump to hasty conclusions about methodological integrity and theoretical confusion because of the discovery of ambiguous or contradictory language. Qualitative health research is a dynamic field, with considerable change and growth during its 20 years or so of popularity. Particularly in the early years, researchers were forced to articulate their methodological choices in a language and form that would pass the review of rather unsympathetic journal editors, peer reviewers, and even dissertation committees (Thorne, 1991). Indeed, the impact of various editorial policies and regulations of the journals in which qualitative health research is commonly published may have had a rather profound influence on the nature and quality of the overall body of research (Aldag & Stearns, 1998). For example, where detail about the research design is insufficient to evaluate the research product fully, it is important to remain aware that the absence of such information may be an outcome of an overenthusiastic edit to conform to a page limit, or even an editorial decision. Although patterns can sometimes be detected in the style of research report that appears in a particular journal, an even subtler factor may be the influence of blind reviewers. As those who have attempted to publish qualitative health research are often aware, such reviewers sometimes insist on including methodological statements that may be incongruous with the researcher's intent, and it is the rare researcher who will withdraw a paper under such circumstances unless the proposed change seriously threatens the integrity of the work. Thus, attention to the culture of research dissemination yields a layer of interpretive analysis that can either clarify or obscure claims relating to what is known about a particular body of research.

THE APPRAISAL OF INDIVIDUAL PRIMARY STUDIES

Meta-method begins with an appraisal of the methodologies of individual primary research reports. This includes a review of the research question, the role of the researcher(s), the sampling procedures, and the data collection procedures for their fit with the stated research method and their influence on the research findings. The specific approach to primary research appraisal of the methods will be developed for each meta-study in accordance with its own particular requirements. In our research, we have found it useful to adapt Burns's (1989) classic claims about methodological congruence so that we can easily identify threats to documentation rigor, procedural rigor, ethical rigor, and auditability (see Appendix A). Using these criteria, we can determine whether the selection of subjects is done in a manner that is appropriate to the research question or whether the researcher role is consistent with the philosophical underpinnings of the method that has been applied.

Some general criteria can be applied to the evaluation of the full range of qualitative methodological approaches. Other criteria are quite specific to the method that has been used. In an ethnographic study, for example, the time invested in fieldwork must be sufficient to capture relevant seasonal, cyclical, or developmental variations within the experience being studied (Wolcott, 1990). Phenomenological research must include evidence that the researcher has bracketed the understandings that might inhibit engaging with experience (Crotty, 1998; Ray, 1994). Other criteria may be relevant to some applications of a particular methodological approach but not others. For example, it would be important to understand that one would expect major differences in the fundamental approach to the research question, to the research participants, and to the processes of data generation between descriptive and interpretive (or European and American) phenomenology (Caelli, 2000). With this complexity in mind, we now turn to a discussion of some salient criteria you may find helpful to consider in your meta-method analysis. Although our list of criteria is far from exhaustive, we hope it will direct you to consider significant issues that may be helpful in appraising the methodological implications of primary research.

THE RESEARCH QUESTION

A review of primary research in a meta-study determines the fit between the research question and what the researcher actually did in the conduct of the study. Generally, research that seeks to investigate the meaning of experiences employs some form of phenomenological method, whereas research questions that pertain to the description of cultural behaviors may be best answered by ethnographic approaches, and process questions may require a grounded theory approach (Morse, 1994).

The choice of qualitative research methods should usually be determined by what the researcher decides is the desired outcome of the research (Stern, 1994). Too often, however, it seems that researchers select a method that is familiar, or that has been previously employed in the discipline, or that will be readily accepted as legitimate inquiry in their opinion. As we have explained, we have often encountered studies in which the fit between the method named and the actual procedures followed was extremely loose. In such cases, it is important for the interpretive analyst to speculate about why this may have occurred. In some instances, it may be reasonable to conclude that the researchers have failed to appreciate the contradictions inherent in their methodological claims. In other instances, it may be that the researchers have thoughtfully modified and adapted conventional approaches to do justice to the research questions they want to ask (Thorne, 1991; Thorne et al., 1997). Careful scrutiny and reflection may reveal that what they report about their actual research process sounds reasonable and that only the label that has been assigned to the method seems contradictory. Again, it may be instructive to reflect on why this may have occurred. For example, because some funders and editors may accept only those reports in which the researcher has used traditional and well-recognized methods, the author may have claimed work to be informed by a tradition that only loosely applies. Although it can be fascinating to speculate about why research is described according to one tradition and not another, a word of caution is also required here. During our years of speculating about why the body of qualitative knowledge is the way it is, we have often developed wild hunches and theories. Only rarely, however, have we actually been able to test them out and confirm that our suspicions were correct. We believe, therefore, that this exercise is often more applicable to raising intriguing questions than to providing tangible answers.

Another consideration relating to the research question is the degree to which it constrains the boundaries of the investigation. For example, some research questions are articulated in such a manner that they make explicit certain parameters of the study. Studies that investigate a particular concept in chronic illness are a case in point. We have noticed that researchers who focus on a particular concept within chronic illness experience (e.g., hope, courage, suffering) may interpret complex aspects of the overall experience within the restricted frame of that concept. The researcher seeking to learn about optimism, for example, may not be sufficiently open to detect evidence of pessimism or despair within the participants' accounts. Thus, clues that appear in verbatim transcriptions or accounts of the participants may lead the meta-method analyst to conclude that the research question has shaped the research process in particular ways and, at times, even predetermined the interpretation that will be possible as the research process evolves.

A related aspect of meta-method analysis is the fit among the research question, the method, and the findings. We have been disturbed to find, for example, research results that claimed authority in subjective experience on the basis of observations or structured interviews. We have also been distressed to find researchers drawing objective conclusions for social or health policy on the basis of data that rely entirely on social construction in a particular interactional context, such as in focus group interviews. On occasions, we have found credible and auditable data analysis followed by interpretations that appear to bear no relationship whatsoever to the actual research but that may have occurred to the researcher during the course of the study. In the chronic illness field, for example, we have often been puzzled by apparent biases and muddiness in the interpretation of research results. In some instances, researchers link data back into the theoretical frameworks of their discipline regardless of whether there is a relevant fit; in others, the results seem to have been skewed by a personal experience with illness. Where conclusions oversimplify complex data (e.g., the claim that breast cancer is best interpreted as a gift, or as an inspiration to personal transformation), we find ourselves reflecting on what the researcher's "real" research question might have been.

THE RESEARCHER AND THE SETTING

A significant aspect of meta-method is investigating how the relationship between the primary researchers and their study participants may have influenced the nature of the research findings. Although feminist theory has clearly alerted us to the impact of such factors as gender in this regard (Anderson, 1991; Smith, 1990), numerous other demographic and behavioral characteristics will directly influence the rapport that is created, the process of data collection that is used, and the nature of the data that are reported. As a social construction, qualitative research data are a product of the researcher as much as the researched. Typically, however, although we document the demographic characteristics of research participants in meticulous detail, it is much less common (except in explicitly critical interpretive social research) to provide an equally thorough report on the researcher.

Depending on their understanding of the relevant social positioning or the ethnicity of the researcher, research subjects will often reveal information in significantly different ways (Lipson, 1989). The disciplinary background of the researcher may also play an important role in shaping the nature of the data. For example, merely identifying yourself as a "nurse researcher" inherently triggers a set of assumptions about what aspects of an experience would be of interest to a nurse; thus, details about the more private bodily functions are often more readily revealed to nurse researchers than to researchers identified as psychologists or sociologists (Thorne, 1991; Thorne & Robinson, 1988).

The researcher's disciplinary background influences not only the participants' assumptions but also the researcher's orientation to what constitutes relevant knowledge. For example, the concept of uncertainty has attracted interest among sociologists, who have sometimes examined it in the chronic illness context, asking such questions as, "How do persons with inflammatory bowel disease experience uncertainty?" Researchers from the applied health professions, in contrast, are more likely to consider uncertainty relevant only to the degree that it shapes experience and coping with the disease (Lawler, 1998). They might choose such research questions as, "What coping strategies do individuals with inflammatory bowel disease use to mediate the effects of uncertainty in living with the disease?" Thus, the social and theoretical positioning of the researcher can shed considerable light on why two apparently similar studies may yield quite different results.

Another issue that may be relevant in relation to the study of meta-method is the role of the researcher in relation to the participants both prior to and during the research study. For example, the health care field includes numerous examples of studies in which the researcher has a relationship with the study participants that occurs in a clinical context. Although the ethical considerations in such a situation pose one particular set of problems, of primary concern to a meta-study researcher is the way this relationship may have affected the nature of the research data. For example, in our diabetes research, we noted that 10 of the 43 studies were conducted by researchers who had taught or were currently teaching these same participants in a diabetes education clinic or program. Without exception, these researchers concluded that diabetes education was crucial to the successful adaptation of persons with diabetes. In contrast, this kind of conclusion was not nearly as prominent in reports by researchers who had a more distant attachment to the clinical context; some did not address this issue at all.

As this illustration also reveals, the setting of the research may also have significance for the meta-method appraisal. In general, studies conducted in hospitals seem more likely to generate findings relevant to the hospital context, and those conducted in communities more often address issues in the family or social context. Thus, it can be important to consider the degree to which the setting may have influenced what was studied and what was found. In our chronic illness work, for example, we have been intrigued by the degree to which the national origin of a piece of research influences the nature of the findings, particularly as they relate to the social and health care context of illness. As McLaughlin and Zeeberg (1993) have reported, understandings about self-care in multiple sclerosis are a case in point. Researchers in Denmark focus their analysis on the process of seeking physician permission to be excused from work but do not inquire about costs incurred by equipment needs, such as wheelchairs. This focus clearly reflects the structure of their health care system and the way it shapes multiple sclerosis experience in that context. Researchers in North America and the United Kingdom, however, are less likely to recognize that their own health care systems have such an impact and often refer to access, cost, and resource issues as if they were universal.

Finally, the setting and context in which the actual data collection took place is another relevant aspect of the method. We have noticed in the chronic illness research, for example, a notable difference in the findings of studies in which the research is conducted in homes rather than in busy clinics. In some instances, data collection reports reveal that participants were interviewed during an extended clinic day, or while they were waiting to return home after a visit to a health care provider, or even during procedures. Not surprisingly, most of the data arising from such studies lacks the breadth and depth that is revealed in other studies conducted in more relaxed or informal settings or over a longer time period. Although the influence of any singular study conducted in this manner may not be particularly important to the meta-method analysis, trends and patterns that develop in the field, including extension and replication of the findings of other researchers, can create a peculiar context in which one kind of disease or condition tends to be studied in one particular manner in contrast with other diseases. In such cases, it is particularly important to be conscious of how the patterns of research over time may have shaped a particular knowledge base deriving from that body of research.

SAMPLING PROCEDURES

Beyond the qualitative research method chosen for a primary research study, certain methodological decisions made by the primary researcher affect the nature of the research findings. One such decision relates to sampling procedures, particularly the theoretical rationale for sampling, the recruitment method for the sample, and the nature of the sample. Samples in qualitative research are generally, but not always, people. For example, ethnological researchers may sample observational units (Morse & Bottorff, 1990), and historical researchers may use documents (Morse, 1994). Whether the samples in primary research studies are clinically derived; medically referred; taken from the registers of specialized clinics, patient education programs, or self-help groups; or voluntary will influence the nature of the research findings (Conrad, 1990). We have found, for example, that most primary researchers in studies of arthritis obtained their samples from lists of clients attending specialized clinics or receiving care from a rheumatologist. These samples can therefore be considered specialized in that many people with arthritis do not use such services. Thus, findings constructed on the basis of this body of work should be understood only as representative of a subset of those who live with the disease; they might, for example, represent those who are so extensively affected that they require more support than a generalist practitioner can provide.

The selection criteria that primary researchers employ influence both the research findings and the theoretical constructions that emerge from the research. We have noticed, for example, that in the area of chronic illness research, most researchers systematically exclude participants who have comorbidities, such as additional chronic diseases. However, investigators rarely provide such thoughtful control for such variables as family violence or poverty; so, findings about chronic illness become conflated with data related to social conditions, and theoretical linkages are suggested without any firm basis for so doing. Although we would not recommend limiting research to participants who have no additional features of interest, it does seem apparent that the researcher's skill at accounting for how the nature of the sample may or may not have influenced the findings becomes important in evaluating the impact of method.

Another element regarding the selection of participants is the fit with the fundamental principles of the research method. Different qualitative research methods direct researchers to different groups of participants. In phenomenological research, for example, findings may be best obtained from individuals who have the experience or from visual displays of human experience, such as art or movies (Morse, 1994). Where the essence of subjective experience is the focus of the inquiry, however, subjects who are particularly analytical or philosophical about their experience may be inappropriate as research participants. In contrast, grounded theory or ethnography may be well suited to research participants who reflect on or raise questions about their situations or contexts. In some instances, the absence of reflexive research participants may cause the researcher to produce rather superficial or concrete conclusions. The size of the sample is also usually determined by the methodological orientation. For example, one individual case would not be sufficient to produce a grounded theory but may provide in-depth data for a case study (Sandelowski, 1995). In general, determination of the sample size should bear some relationship to the researcher's claims about what is being investigated and for what purpose. Thus, large samples to study intensive and highly personalized experiences might be considered as inappropriate as small samples to generate claims about common patterns or themes within a phenomenon. No matter the nature of the sample, the primary research study should have sufficient sample size to permit the researcher to make some claims in relation to the research question and be small enough to allow in-depth study of individual cases, such that the details are not lost within the general categories used to express those claims (Sandelowski, 1995).

Another issue of concern in meta-method is the congruence between the actual sampling procedures and the purpose of the research. This factor is particularly evident in grounded theory research, in which the principles of theoretical sampling are integral to the method. Theoretical sampling requires that the researcher determine in an ongoing manner what types of participants are needed to answer the research question and to test emerging hypotheses in the data analysis. It derives from the assumption that, to generate theory about basic social process, it is essential to seek maximal variation within those processes. We have noted that although researchers often use the term *theoretical sampling* to describe their approach, there may be little evidence that this has occurred. In some instances, an entirely convenient sample has been "theoretically sampled" by extracting individual quotes or observations within a data set. Further, many researchers fail to account for the negative cases and outliers within their data in the theoretical claims they produce. Similarly, we have noted a range of interpretations of the idea of maximal variation. In many instances, samples vary only in relation to such standardized and traditional factors as age and gender. Factors central to chronic illness experience, such as time from diagnosis and degree of disability, may be completely ignored. Often, either phenomenal or theoretical variation is considered (Sandelowski, 1995), but not both. As would be expected, such sampling strategies powerfully influence whether data interpretation seems skewed or biased in comparison with primary research reports in which the samples reflect more variance.

Despite our observations from our chronic illness research, we remain convinced that there is no inherently right way to create an ideal research sample. Meta-method does permit us, however, to pose questions that illuminate the impact of sampling decisions on the process and product of the inquiry. We can ask such questions as, How has this method of sampling influenced the findings? What are the limitations of this sampling method? What is the demographic profile (e.g., age, gender, level of education, ethnicity) of those who have been studied? and Who have not been studied and why? Each of these questions may lead us to understand in new ways the nature of the knowledge derived from these studies.

DATA COLLECTION TECHNIQUES

The method of data collection is influential in determining the nature of the research findings and the emergent theory that is produced. Singular retrospective, open-ended interviews, for example, have been a popular data collection strategy in the area of chronic illness. The quality of data derived from such interviews is entirely dependent on the participants' ability to recall pertinent incidents and situations and on the researcher's ability to create a relationship and environment conducive to the participants' recall and full disclosure. In our chronic illness meta-study, we were able to compare the nature of research data in primary studies that used multiple interviews with the nature of data in studies that used single interviews. We found the quality of data in multiple interview research to be generally much greater both in depth and in breadth. Researchers in such studies identified more negative cases and outliers, and in many cases the complexity of emergent theory was considerably more advanced.

The interview questions and the techniques of observation are important in determining the nature of research findings. We have noticed, for example, that many researchers posed interview questions that directed the participants to describe their experience in specific ways. For example, a researcher who was purportedly studying the general impact of chronic illness asked questions only about the losses experienced in living with a chronic disease. In that study, no participants responded that the illness had any positive outcomes, such as a renewed sense of self, as has been reported by other researchers. The researcher's conclusion—that living with chronic illness was experienced as a series of losses—therefore came as no surprise.

The interviewing style and skill of the researcher is also a factor in determining the quality and scope of the research data. Analyzing verbatim material, such as is often included in research reports, for example, allows one to develop relevant hunches about interviewing style and the content it produces. Some researchers instill confidence better than others; some lead the interview more than others (Angen, 2000). At times in the chronic illness meta-study, we could almost "hear" the voice of the researcher in the research report. At other times, the data were reported in such a stilted fashion that we wondered whether the researchers had been able to establish any rapport with their participants. Thus, the lines of inquiry that are pursued and the kinds of data that are triggered in an interview process may be markedly different from one researcher to another, and insight about such researcher effects will be important to a more general interpretation of knowledge in the field.

OVERALL APPRAISAL OF PRIMARY STUDIES

As in the appraisal of the individual primary research studies, the overall appraisal of the body of work with meta-method includes a review of the kinds of research questions, methodological orientations, researcher roles, sampling procedures, and data collection procedures that characterize the body of qualitative research in a particular field. In this step, it is a good idea to develop tables whereby researchers can compare and contrast the primary studies efficiently. We have constructed tables, for example, including the nature of the participants according to number, gender, age, ethnicity, and other attributes, as well as the inclusion and exclusion criteria used and the type of sampling procedure (e.g., purposive, nomination, snowball). Summarizing aspects of the method into such a table enables identification of themes and patterns within the overall body of research that may not otherwise be immediately apparent. In our chronic illness meta-study, for example, we discovered that most qualitative cardiac research has been conducted with male samples, whereas women are disproportionately represented in the studies of most other chronic diseases. We also developed tables to summarize findings about research methods, research questions, researcher and setting, and data collection techniques. In so doing, we noted that narrative analysis approaches were far more commonly applied to the study of multiple sclerosis and HIV/AIDS than to any other equally disruptive chronic condition.

THE RESEARCH METHOD

The overall appraisal can result in an understanding of how the use of research methods has changed over time, in specific disciplines, and among specific researchers. Because certain researchers tend to focus on specific areas of inquiry and may prefer certain methods, the influence of specific methods may be particularly apparent in certain fields of inquiry. The preference of researchers for certain methods is understandable. Graduate students master a research method to become marketable and to gain entrance to the profession (Szmatka & Lovaglia, 1996). Available methods have differing levels of appeal to researchers, depending on the researcher's personality, ideology, discipline, experience, and access to mentorship. Consequently, some qualitative researchers become wedded to particular research methods and are known as ethnographers, grounded theorists, and the like. As a meta-study researcher, you must have as your objective the posing of such questions as, "How has the predominance of a research method within a specific discipline or group of researchers affected their research findings and the way they interpret the phenomenon under study?"

The nature of the research methods in the area is significant in the overall appraisal, particularly regarding its descriptive or interpretive properties or both. If the majority of the research in a particular area is descriptive, for example, the more interpretive or normative considerations of that phenomenon will be missing. As a result, the body of knowledge that accumulates in that field may have limited utility for practitioners.

THE RESEARCH QUESTION

Meta-method allows analysts to consider such issues as what questions researchers ask in a particular field of study and why they ask such questions. Are patterns and themes evident within the kinds of questions that attract considerable research attention in the field and those that seem not to have been asked? Knowing the logic by which the research questions are justified may be helpful in making sense of how they may have influenced the overall body of knowledge. You might consider whether the research questions that tend to be asked are grounded in the same kinds of knowledge or whether clinical or theoretical questions are more prominent in driving the investigation of that particular phenomenon. In essence, the meta-method researcher approaches the body of research armed with the question, "So what?"

Although qualitative health research is not universally designed to create practical knowledge, it is important to discern the contribution of the research question to the discipline or field of study, including what researchers in a given discipline may have neglected or confused. In our chronic illness meta-study, for example, we found studies in which the researchers sought to answer how individuals adapt to illness by asking questions like, "What strategies do persons with chronic illness employ to cope with a chronic illness?" This kind of question has produced a substantial body of knowledge about the cognitive strategies that individuals with chronic illness use. Because of the way such questions are typically framed, however, we know much less about the emotional content of participants' experience and how emotional reactions might influence their cognitive responses to the chronic disease. Thus, consideration of the kinds of questions asked can be informative in alerting the researcher to the particular relevance of specific research that may have addressed a gap or limitation within the field.

THE RESEARCHER AND SETTING

Tabulating the analysis of individual research reports in relation to the role of the researcher and the setting of research may provide valuable insights about how research has been conducted and where. For example, because most primary research into illness experience is conducted in urban areas, it is difficult to know how relevant such findings would be for understanding the illness experience of those in more geographically isolated or rural areas where access to services is more restricted. Although conclusions about the influence of these factors on the research findings must be made with considerable caution, it is often revealing to compare and contrast the nature of the findings that arise in relation to the researcher's gender, academic discipline, or nationality. For example, we were intrigued to note that male researchers in the chronic illness primary studies often focused their research on the social structures that influence the experience of living with a chronic illness, whereas female researchers tended to focus on the meaning of the experience. On further investigation, we discovered that the vast majority of the male qualitative health researchers were sociologists, grounded in a discipline strongly oriented toward the analysis of social structures. Thus, the interaction between gender and discipline would be difficult to determine, and we recognized how easy it might be to jump to conclusions on the basis of our preliminary hunches. This example further alerted us to the value of creating processes and strategies by which to engage in an ongoing dialectic with the body of work to understand its nature as fully as possible.

One step that we believe is crucial in an overall appraisal is locating the primary studies by the political or geographic regions they represent. For example, Lawler (1998) cautions that published nursing research most often comes from researchers in the United States or is published in U.S. nursing journals. She suggests that we need to be reflexive about how the "intellectual and scholarly tradition" (p. 106) of American researchers has determined how research will be conducted. In our chronic illness meta-study, the predominance of North American researchers is incontestable. As we reflected on this, we began to wonder about the degree to which the individualism inherent in U.S. social ideology may explain, in part, the emphasis in the research literature on individual rather than social or familial experience in chronic illness. Certainly, other national ideological perspectives may have equally compelling influences on a body of research. When the weight of the primary research studies reflects a particular nation's ways of being and knowing, the meta-study researcher needs to question the effect on the understanding of the phenomenon under study that has been generated from research in the area.

SAMPLING PROCEDURES

A review of the samples of primary research included in a meta-method will reveal both who has and who has not been included in investigations of the phenomenon under study. This revelation may lead to the identification of crucial omissions in the body of knowledge available. Clearly, it is not possible for researchers to include all types and variations of people and situations in any single research project. The tendency, however, is for researchers to select samples that are easy to access and interview. Consequently, when the body of work is considered, some significant populations may be missed. For example, in the study of stroke, samples have typically included only those patients who are able to speak clearly; thus, the subjective experience of aphasic stroke patients is not adequately documented. When the nature of the sample is recognized, the inherent limitations in what is currently known become apparent.

DATA COLLECTION TECHNIQUES

The comparison of research methodologies used for primary research is helpful in exposing the predominant data collection techniques that have been used in the body of research, as well as in directing the meta-study researcher to data collection techniques that have been neglected or forgotten. Meta-method reveals the preferences of researchers for specific data collection techniques and how these have influenced the nature of the research findings in the area. Our analysis of chronic illness research demonstrated that although qualitative researchers often write about creative and innovative data collection techniques, such as the review of photographs and historical documents, the popularity of interviewing and participant observation remains overwhelming.

The overall appraisal also reveals the particulars of the predominant data collection techniques. We have noted, for example, that techniques for gathering interview data have changed in recent years. Whereas many early qualitative health researchers used a one-time interview to gather data about experiences in living with chronic illness, more recent researchers are increasingly using multiple and focus group interviews. Because we have observed trends in the nature of research findings as they have shifted during the same time period, we were prompted to speculate about the significance of changing data collection techniques in relation to the research findings. Would individual interviews tend to produce a more superficial and socially constructed interpretation of living with a chronic disease than would more intensive interviewing methods? Would certain kinds of data be more prominent in findings from studies relying on focus groups than on individual interviews? Because focus group theory assumes that participants will be more readily able to access and communicate information about themselves by virtue of interaction with those who have had similar experiences, it will be informative to grapple with how that principle will play out in actual practice. For example, we might ask whether aspects of illness experiences that are more "socially unacceptable" (e.g., continence mishaps, bodily odors) are more or less likely to arise in an individual private interview or in a discussion with fellow travelers.

CONCLUSION

Meta-study researchers who conduct meta-method are reciprocally engaged in the methodological foundations of the body of research they attempt to analyze. The body of primary research serves as a case study of the prevailing ideas and techniques over time, framed by the disciplinary, geographical, and ideological contexts within which it arose. Meta-method reveals these different visions of research methodology and discloses both their liberating and limiting aspects. Meta-method can be a challenging analytic enterprise; it requires considerable methodological knowledge on the part of the meta-study researcher and may offer few definitive answers in comparison with the number of questions it raises. As Sandelowski and colleagues (1997) correctly remind us, it is easier to take things apart than to attempt to synthesize the parts to add to our understanding of a phenomenon under study. We believe, however, that the promise of meta-method overrides its challenges. It offers a means to introduce new interpretations and techniques to our qualitative research approaches and adds to our understanding of the methodological complexities inherent in investigating health and illness phenomena.

6

META-THEORY

Meta-theory is a critical exploration of the theoretical frameworks or lenses that have provided direction to research and to researchers, as well as the theory that has arisen from research in a particular field of study (Neufeld, 1994). In this context, *theory* is understood as "a system of interrelated propositions that should enable phenomena to be described, explained, predicted, and controlled" (Duldt & Griffin, 1985, p. 1). The procedures of meta-theory as outlined by Ritzer (1990, 1992b) and adapted by ourselves include (a) identifying major cognitive paradigms and schools of thought that are represented in both the theoretical frameworks and the emerging theory of selected research reports; (b) relating the theory to the larger sociocultural, historical, and political context; and (c) deconstructing the implications of significant assumptions underlying specific theories.

THE PURPOSE

Ritzer (1992b) differentiates between three main types of meta-theorizing. He variously describes it as (a) a means to attain a deeper understanding of what a theory entails, (b) a technique to develop new theory to explain the phenomenon under study, and (c) a process for developing overarching theory that includes two or more theories. From our perspective, the essential purpose of meta-theory is analysis of the implications of theory on the body of research so that the extant theory can be critically interpreted, tested, and even developed, by using meta-synthesis, into new theory.

Meta-theory offers a systematic means of understanding and evaluating the theory that drives and arises from qualitative research. It focuses our attention on the theoretical traditions and analytic frameworks underlying our research. Ritzer (1990) claims that what distinguishes meta-theory from other analytic enterprises is not so much the processes involved as the end-products of such work. To illustrate, Hamalainen's (1989) meta-theory examination of social pedagogy in the discipline of social work resulted in recommendations in relation to the nature of the competencies and skills that should be taught in social work education. Similarly, Ferguson, Ferguson, and Taylor's (1992) critical analysis of the theoretical underpinnings of disability theory as applied to disability research resulted in reconceptualizing disability as a social construction rather than as the objectifiable, disembodied reality that characterized earlier interpretations. On the basis of this analysis, these researchers were able to encourage researchers in this field of study to adopt research approaches, using an interpretive paradigm, that were more congruent with understanding disability as a social construction.

THE NATURE OF THEORY IN META-THEORY

Meta-theory involves the analysis of primary studies for the implications of their theoretical orientations. As McKenna (1997) points out, numerous linkages between theory and research can be detected within the qualitative health research literature. These include the following:

- *Theory testing research,* or primary research studies in which researchers attempt to determine the accuracy of the theory in depicting a phenomenon under study, such as a study in which a theory of self-care is investigated by interviewing persons who have experienced a particular illness.

- *Theory generating research,* whereby theory is inductively generated from the primary research data, such as a primary study that results in a grounded theory of suffering.

- *Theory evaluating research,* whereby a theory is evaluated for its effects on a particular population of participants, such as a primary research in which the implementation of Orem's (1997) self-care theory on a hospital unit is evaluated in terms of the clients' perceptions of their hospital experience.

- *Theory framed research,* whereby a theory is used to frame the primary research study, such as the use of a theory of coping to provide focus to a study of the experience of living with chronic back pain.

Although some of these applications of theory might seem more applicable to quantitative than qualitative research, we encountered all of these forms of theory-research linkage in the primary qualitative studies we analyzed for our chronic illness meta-study project.

In addition, it is useful to consider that various kinds of theories can be subject to analysis in meta-theory. For example, *grounded theory* is often considered that which is generated inductively from grounded data (Lincoln & Guba, 1985; Strauss, 1995) and may be presented as a theory arising from the research findings. *Substantive or midrange theory* is that which may be used to orient the research toward particular concepts (e.g., hope, uncertainty, spirituality) or relationships among those concepts (Steeves et al., 1996). *Grand theories* are those overarching theoretical claims that reflect a more "general orientation toward reality" (Steeves et al., 1996, p. 209) and may be used implicitly or explicitly as an epistemological position from which all aspects of the research are guided. These theories can be applied to various aspects of the research enterprise in distinct ways. They can shape the concepts with which the phenomenon under study is described, the operational definitions by which they are applied, and the propositions that explain their predicted relationships with other concepts and constructs (Chinn & Kramer, 1995).

The relationship between theory and research is complex and varies considerably between disciplines and scholarly perspectives. Within the social sciences, the very nature of scholarship is inherently theory driven (Reason, 1996; Weinstein & Weinstein, 1992). In contrast, theory may be more tangentially related to knowledge development within the health sciences and in some instances is used simply to anchor new inquiries within scholarship in a way that legitimates qualitative research as science (Sandelowski, 1993b). Thus, the theories that are used and the way that those theories are used are both fodder for the meta-theory analyst.

As is the case with meta-method, detecting the role of theory in qualitative research is not always easy, and the explicit theories on which a study is founded may not be stated as such in the research report (Sandelowski, 1993b). Some forms of qualitative research demand a thorough theoretical positioning of each new study; others encourage the researcher to take a fresher and more unbiased perspective. Further, authors of published reports are not always frank about the way their theoretical locations have shaped their research questions, designs, interpretations, and conclusions. For example, we know of numerous instances in which a study claiming no particular theoretical orientation concludes with a strong endorsement for a singular theoretical conclusion without having apparently examined alternative options. As with methodological choices, researchers may have several reasons for favoring one theory over another. These reasons may be associated with such factors as disciplinary traditions, available mentors, academic pressure within certain departments, or the apparent simplicity of a particular theoretical option. However, they may also reflect theoretical allegiances or camps of scholarship in which adherence to a particular way of theorizing ensures credibility or acceptance among certain communities.

Just as language selection within the design description may reveal methodological perspectives that are not made explicit in the text, certain cues and signals often reveal the influence that bodies of theory or specific theorists have had on a particular piece of qualitative research. The most obvious is the reference list in which the bibliographic sources are listed. We have found it highly informative to consider the relationship between what the researcher has read (or not read) and how the results of a study may have been influenced. For example, within nursing research, one can find numerous examples of published studies in which the text of the research report suggests an attitude of openness to theoretical options but in which the reference list reveals an almost exclusive reliance on the writings of particular nursing theorists. In general, as might be anticipated, researchers who read in the narrower fields often seem more likely to produce the more predictable research results. Because most journal editors insist on limiting reference lists to those sources specifically cited and excluding those that may have had a more general influence on the author's thinking, however, some discretion must be used to avoid leaping to conclusions on the basis of the source list alone. Thus, meta-theory offers a distinct analytic strategy for making sense of a body of research by examining the ways theories operate within it and influence the nature and structure of the knowledge it represents.

THE INITIAL PROCEDURES

The initial procedures of meta-theory entail reading primary research reports thoroughly, noting the theoretical perspective used and any emergent theory, and deciding which additional theories may have had significant influence on the primary research. The most significant step in meta-theory is a careful and thoughtful reading of the primary research reports to identify the various ways in which theory may have influenced their shape and nature. In many instances, repeated readings, comparing the texts of various research reports with one another, may be necessary to developing sensitivity for the cues and signals by which theory can be recognized. Such intensive reading will often be necessary to distinguish a primary researcher's theoretical claims from any theoretical perspectives that may have crept into the report without conscious intent. Further, the meta-theorist cannot assume that the researcher's overt statements about which theory has been used and how it has been used will be accurate or useful to the analysis.

In many cases, theoretical foundations can also be indirectly discerned in the meta-theory analysis process. Cues like reliance on terms such as *stress* and *coping* may indicate an implicit reliance on the work of such prominent theorists as Lazarus and Folkman (1984), whereas terms such as *adaptation* may reveal an orientation toward a different set of ideas, such as those advanced by Helson (1964), Dubos (1965), or Selye (1976). Although many authors will confirm their reliance on such ideas through reference citations, those who do not may either be unaware of the degree to which such ideas might shape their research or assume that such ideas are sufficiently general knowledge not to require citation. Even though those who attribute their ideas to specific theorists may be more helpful in pointing a meta-theory analyst in the appropriate direction, generalizations about how overt and covert theory influence each study will have to be individually derived and defended. Beyond scrutinizing individual studies for the degree to which they account for the influence of theoretical claims on their investigations, however, it is useful to be aware of the way certain theoretical perspectives can often come to dominate research in a particular field. Most researchers build the case for their own studies on those that are most closely linked to the research question, and thus some theoretical influences may reach considerably beyond any particular piece of research.

From a thorough reading of the primary research reports, you can summarize what you have found by documenting in a table format what theories have been used or emerge from the research. This significant step may lead to salient insights. For example, when we looked at the number of chronic illness studies that had used stigma as an overarching theory or whose authors had concluded that their research findings supported the theory of stigma, we were struck by some interesting interpretations. Many researchers who referred to the theory of stigma conducted their research mainly in the early 1980s and applied it in the investigation of experience with such conditions as disability, epilepsy, inflammatory bowel disease, and multiple sclerosis. This fact led us to wonder why stigma lost favor as a theoretical framework for investigating these same conditions in the 1990s. Our analysis led us to the recognition that some of what might have been interpreted as a response to stigma in the 1980s was reframed as a normalization strategy by researchers in the 1990s. As well, we recognized that the early researchers had focused on stigma as it pertained to recognized societal discomfort with the visibility of these conditions. As HIV/AIDS took over prominence in the stigma arena, the social aspect of the original conditions may have seemed less interesting. Further, we began to wonder whether increasing social and political consciousness in relation to the rights and needs of those with disabilities may have made researchers less enthusiastic about documenting the experience of stigma. In keeping with a changing social climate, researchers may have been reluctant to document disabilities or disadvantages for groups who wanted to be represented by their abilities and strengths. Thus, we were able to raise some challenges relating to why and how certain theories such as stigma may have held considerable prominence in various fields of study at various times. By noticing and documenting shifts in theoretical applications, we could begin to question what external social factors might have explained these shifts.

PROCEDURES FOR THEORY ANALYSIS

Some valiant efforts have been made to challenge well-established grand and substantive theories throughout the past few decades. For example, Diederiks and Bal's (1997) meta-theory analysis of the illness-trajectory framework (Strauss & Glaser, 1975) has illuminated the contradiction that arises in the theoretical aspirations of this framework. It is classified both as an interactionist theory of chronic illness, in which the work of chronic illness is seen as an emergent phenomenon that defies planning, and as a practical imperative for the care of persons with chronic illness, implying organizational planning and design. Although meta-theory may help transform the way specific theories are understood and applied, Neufeld (1994) warns meta-theorists that this transformation can evoke criticism and hostility resulting from resistance to changing one's ways of thinking about a particular phenomenon.

A critical meta-theory analysis of the theories that shape a body of research may entail these steps:

1. Identifying the major cognitive paradigms that underlie the theory

2. Identifying the assumptions underlying the theory

3. Examining the historical evolution of the theory, including how it has changed over time, adaptations to its original conception, and significant landmarks in its evolution

4. Determining how the sociocultural, disciplinary, and political context may have influenced the selection of theoretical frameworks or their interpretation of research findings to support a particular theory

5. Evaluating the quality of the selected theory

IDENTIFYING MAJOR PARADIGMS

Major paradigms or schools of thought that underlie particular theoretical frameworks shape the way the phenomena under study are investigated and understood. For this reason, highlighting the paradigmatic origins of the selected theory and speculating about their influence on research within the field of study are important. For example, a theoretical perspective of gender relations in which the researcher claims feminist standpoint epidemiological roots might result in research in which the aim is to describe oppression of women. Such research might involve only female participants and present gender as a social construction, negating biophysical accounts of human sexuality or manhood/womanhood (Grassie, 1996). In contrast, if the underlying theoretical perspective was feminist postmodernism, assumptions about privilege according to gender might be deconstructed, both male and female participants might be included, and the aim might be to determine ways in which people use ideas about oppression in making sense of their unique experiences (Grassie, 1996). If the research was grounded in an explicitly critical feminist social theory, however, it might be expected to uncover covert dynamics associated with power imbalances and involve an emancipatory response of some sort toward interrupting and correcting those embedded power imbalances between genders. Thus, subtle differences in the nature of theorizing can sometimes make significant differences in what is studied, how it is studied, and why it is studied.

The identification of major paradigms involves making some suppositions about how the underlying theoretical framework has influenced the choice of the research question(s) and approaches to data collection and analysis, as well as ultimately the nature of the project toward which the individual piece of research is directed. In our chronic illness meta-study, for example, we determined that Parsons's (1951) sick role theory defined illness as deviance and the health care professional as the "social control agent" (Conrad, 1990, p. 1259). Consequently, primary researchers who used this as a theoretical framework focused on individuals' experiences as patients within their encounters with health care professionals, rather than on the total experience of living with chronic illness. They used interviews and observation techniques to capture what occurs within patient-professional encounters but did not interrogate the significance of these encounters to the individual with chronic illness. Although this body of research has provided valuable insights about how individuals with chronic illness experience their relationships with health care professionals, it gives a limited understanding of what it is like to live with a chronic illness. Interestingly, when Parsons's sick role theory lost favor among academics in the 1980s and 1990s, many researchers appeared to lose sight of the powerful influence that health care professionals' values and attitudes toward them could have on the everyday experience of persons living with chronic illness. Thus, in this instance, both the presence and the absence of certain theoretical perspectives in the research explain something of the angle of focus on the phenomenon under study.

The identification of major paradigms or schools of thought that underlie the selected theory requires that the meta-theorist be well versed in the origins of various theories in the field of study or have access to resources that will assist him or her in attaining that knowledge. Some excellent available resources help in locating the theoretical underpinnings of nursing theories, as well as in tracing the origins of their concepts within the social and life sciences (e.g., Chinn & Kramer, 1995; Fawcett & Downs, 1992; Meleis, 1997). Introductory texts and systematic reviews in psychology, sociology, and anthropology can be a useful beginning point for locating the history, origins, and influence of certain theoretical positions within the social sciences (e.g., Ritzer, 1992b). Another resource to consider in this step of meta-theory is your network of colleagues in other disciplines who are experts on theoretical development within that discipline or who have extensive knowledge about specific theories. In our chronic illness meta-study, for example, we encountered one theory of disability whose relevance in shaping research was not clear to us. A social work colleague was helpful in pointing us to appropriate references in the field and in explaining the paradigmatic foundations of that theory. Because meta-theorists will almost inevitably have to stretch their analyses beyond the confines of the theoretical positions within which they have been trained, the use of these basic overview resources, as well as access to a wide range of colleague consultants, can be an important asset to the meta-theory process.

As you engage in the process of meta-theory, do not be reticent about approaching experts or authors directly for theoretical explanations. The Internet provides an extremely helpful mechanism for quickly locating addresses of experts through academic institutions or for seeking clarification from primary authors without committing them to the time involved in a formal consultation. We have been delighted with the enthusiastic responses from many such experts, for whom an e-mail exchange about their favorite topic may be a pleasure rather than an intrusion. Some individuals we first contacted this way have subsequently become colleagues, and our virtual discussions of shared interests have continued. Thus, we are convinced that this kind of collegial exchange, when handled respectfully and responsibly, can be mutually beneficial.

IDENTIFYING UNDERLYING ASSUMPTIONS

In many ways, it is prudent to assume a devil's advocate position in meta-theorizing, particularly in examining theories that have evolved from research findings. Brookfield (1991) refers to this as "reflective skepticism." The meta-study researcher must identify and challenge the assumptions of the theories that are revealed in research reports, including examining how the context of the research report (e.g., the nature of the sample, the research question, the researcher's choice of theoretical perspective) influenced the theoretical claims that arose from the findings. A useful adjunct to this analytic step is to explore and imagine alternative ways that might have been used to make sense of the research findings. For example, when we examined the conclusions of various research reports in the diabetes study, we found it informative that many authors assumed that self-care decision making arose from body listening and that attention to cues one's body produced was adaptive and constructive. We wondered how the researchers framed their questions in relation to this phenomenon and whether they thought to inquire about the possibility that body listening might not always be effective or whether it might at times have untoward social or psychological consequences. By interrogating the provided conclusions against other interpretations that might have been possible, we were able to raise questions concerning the uncritical acceptance of certain theoretical truths. Such "truths" might in turn have influenced the conclusions of studies conducted by several different authors. This analytic process allowed us to shift in our interpretation from assuming that the similarities between studies strengthened their collective truth value toward recognizing the possibility of a systematic influence of one kind of theorizing on a generation of findings. In this way, meta-theorizing sets analyses about the factors influencing conclusions in contrast with the collective weight of those conclusions, thus permitting meta-study researchers to extend their interpretations beyond the obvious.

Assumptions underlying specific theories are not always clearly stated; they must often be surmised from what is included in the written report.

Commonly, the assumptions underlying theories in qualitative research can be extrapolated from analysis of the way theory shapes aspects of the research design. For example, a researcher might ask the research question, "What is the nature of support for persons living with end-stage renal failure?" The data might then be constructed by requesting that research participants describe who gives support and how it is given. Any theory of support that arises from such research would be based on the following assumptions: (a) Support can be captured in the descriptions of those experiencing it; (b) support arises from an active, rather than a passive, stance (someone has to do something for the person to experience support); and (c) the perception of support is a personally constructed, rather than a socially constructed, phenomenon. Although these assumptions are neither right nor wrong, they do define the boundaries of the emergent theory in explaining the support experience of living with this particular health challenge. Such a theory might not shed light on the more spiritual or existential elements of support, but it might reduce the abstraction of support to those tangible instances when a supportive action can be articulated, and it might completely overlook the possibility of sociocultural expectations and norms that shape shared understandings of whether support ought to be provided and how it should be demonstrated.

Ferguson and his colleagues (1992) indicate that the ultimate pragmatic test of the underlying assumptions of a theory is how these assumptions affect the lives of those who are studied. For example, a common assumption underlying the substantive theory about clients' participation as equal partners in decisions about their disease management is that equal participation will lead to optimal health outcomes. Thorne and Paterson (1998) question this assumption in their critique of the theory, postulating that such an assumption has resulted in health care practitioners who assume that participation is the ideal for all clients. Consequently, client partnership is imposed on clients regardless of their cultural, developmental, and personal needs to the contrary. Ironically, this assumption then provides a form of justification for unequal service in health care, because clients comfortable with partnership also come to be understood as most deserving. Thus, a creative challenge to the assumptions underlying theory within a body of qualitative research may raise questions about the field, as well as propose possible answers.

IDENTIFYING THE INFLUENCE OF CONTEXT

Meta-theory requires an attentiveness to its historical context in order to reflect on the origins and evolution of theoretical traditions and analytical frameworks. At times, this task may be rather straightforward, as when the theory under study has been derived from a primary research study that is also included in the meta-study. At other times, the determination of context may entail considerable further reading and exploration to track down theoretical claims and linkages.

Although meta-theory does not produce a complete historical analysis within a specific field of study, it does entail a critical analysis of why and how certain theories have evolved or changed over time. For example, meta-theory enables the researcher to track various periods within the history of studying any particular substantive area and to identify the relevant macro-micro distinctions, the theoretical divisions that have occurred, and the conflicts that have arisen between and among researchers about the interpretation and use of certain theories.

An example can be found in Crossley's (1998) historical analysis of various theoretical interpretations of illness as they have applied to HIV/AIDS experience. Although Parsons's (1951) sick role theory had been popular in earlier interpretations of chronic illness experience, it was later roundly criticized as the source of assumptions that the sick person was passive in relationships with health care professionals. Empowerment theory, in which the individual with the disease was viewed as an active participant in such relationships, was adopted by many researchers in the 1990s as an alternative theoretical perspective that justified active involvement for both the patient and the professional in these relationships. More recently, however, researchers have recognized that sick role theory may well provide an important social perspective that explains aspects of HIV/AIDS experience not otherwise explainable. Further, they acknowledge that empowerment theory fails to allow for the notion that persons with illnesses may actually have dependency needs (Crossley, 1998). Thus, the shifting trends in what is considered "politically correct" in interpreting research findings can be tracked through questioning why certain theories are brought into play to explain findings at certain times in our theoretical history and why, at other times, they are ignored.

The broader sociocultural and political contexts in which theory emerges can sometimes be determined through a critical analysis of the influences on theory development at the time the research was conducted. This analysis requires an attentiveness to history, politics, and society "in a comparative frame" (Neufeld, 1994). An example of this kind of meta-theory is Hamalainen's (1989) analysis of social pedagogy. Hamalainen argues that this approach to education has been embraced by German social workers because it fits their ideological and historical views of what is right and good. Theory should also be examined in the light of the macrocontext (Ritzer, 1990)—that is, what was happening in the sociocultural and political setting that may have had an impact on the way the theory evolved and was interpreted? The meta-theory researcher should ask how the theoretical efforts to deal with the phenomenon relate to one another and contribute to the broader understanding of the micro-macro integration of the phenomenon. It would also be important to question the relationship between this work and previous attempts to develop a theoretical framework to explain the phenomenon.

In our chronic illness meta-study research, for example, we asked such questions as, "How have shifting understandings of 'political correctness' affected the theoretical foundations of research?" Examples of the way prevailing social attitudes about appropriate and socially responsible research seem to influence the theoretical orientation of some of the studies we have reviewed are (a) the reluctance of many researchers to mention disquieting terms such as *social class* and (b) the assumption by many that research on or about women ought to reflect an explicitly feminist orientation.

We also asked how general "public discourse" about issues influences the theoretical perspectives that researchers adopt in their inquiries. For instance, the public discourses that arose after the Rodney King affair and the O. J. Simpson trial are examples of situations that enter the public domain and influence how researchers frame social processes such as racism and family violence. Similarly, the public disclosure of chronic illness among prominent public figures such as Michael J. Fox (Parkinson's disease), Montel Williams (multiple sclerosis), and Magic Johnson (HIV infection) often has a remarkable impact on the social constructions of such illness experiences, shaping the way individuals understand their own stories, as well as the way researchers interpret them. Observing such shifts in public discourse, we ask ourselves whether there are theoretical perspectives and underlying assumptions that researchers rarely contest because to do so would risk the wrath of their reading audiences. For example, when television talk show host Oprah Winfrey teaches America certain ways of understanding human relationships, such as the axiom that love should never hurt, such messages may remain virtually unchallenged by researchers.

An excellent example of how meta-theory can contribute to an understanding of the social and political influences on prevailing theory about a phenomenon under study is Orr's (1997) analysis of how and why the theory about race and ethnicity has changed since the 1950s. Although his focus was on literature within the discipline of sociology, Orr's historical and textual analysis of the theoretical shifts that occurred over time in the fields of race and ethnicity points to the influence of social movements such as the women's and antiwar movements in determining the "categorical and paradigmatic underpinnings" (p. 31) of sociological theory. In a similar manner, the human/civil rights movements of the 1960s and 1970s may have created a focus on disadvantage and brought to light the inequities that exist in the treatment of persons with chronic illness. The era during which Goffman (1963) put forth his theories on stigma, for example, reflected the aftermath of the Cuban missile crisis and the general unrest within U.S. society that was characteristic of the time. In contrast, the activism of persons with HIV/AIDS beginning in the mid-1980s was more typically interpreted as a normalizing strategy than as a response to stigma. In the context of those rather different times, researchers may have been reluctant to enter into the political conflict that might have ensued had their interpretations focused on social attitudes instead of effective coping.

EVALUATING THE QUALITY OF THE THEORY

The quality of the theory should be examined in meta-theory because such an evaluation often reveals the limitations, strengths, and ambiguities inherent in a theory. Several sources of theory analysis are available to meta-theory researchers for this purpose. In our chronic illness meta-study, we used Lenski's (1988) standards for theory construction.

These standards alerted us to whether or not the theory contained un-ambiguous concepts, articulated clearly identified relationships between and among the concepts, and included theoretical propositions that were empirically testable (Cohen, 1994; Zhao, 1996).

We conducted a meta-theory analysis of quality of life as a conceptual-ization that has provided a theoretical perspective for several of the pri-mary research studies in our chronic illness meta-study. Using Lenski's criteria, we determined that many concepts and constructs of this theory were unclear and held different meanings in different contexts. This was most often evident when we contrasted the elements of the theory with the research findings. For example, because many researchers may as-sume that the presence of pain inevitably diminishes quality of life, they may not consider the possibility that some persons with chronic illness learn to live with constant pain and view themselves as having a high quality of life. Because a subjective orientation to defining pain has be-come politically correct during recent years within health care circles (e.g., "Pain is whatever the patient says it is"), persons with chronic pain who are able to surmount the impact of pain on their quality of life may be understood as no longer experiencing pain.

Functional integrity is another central characteristic of quality of life according to many theorists. Because it is often defined in terms of the ability to do what persons without the disease can do, researchers may not recognize that, in chronic illness, functional integrity may be re-framed as the ability to do what is possible within the confines of illness. In the analysis of quality of life, we found many other theories about such concepts as suffering, courage, and health that shared similar prop-erties under certain conditions. The relationships among these theories were not well developed, and so the meaning of the concepts they shared was difficult to interpret. For example, although many research-ers interpret suffering as an indicator of a poor quality of life, this link-age does not account for some ideas often considered within theories of suffering, such as the reconstruction of self (Dildy, 1992). If suffering produces transformation to a more valued identity, for example, can it possibly be indicative of a poor quality of life? This exercise enabled us to work out compatibilities and incompatibilities between various theoretical claims that have been used to describe chronic illness expe-rience. It also forced us to use caution in our analysis of research find-ings, because typically a researcher would tend to draw only on those theoretical perspectives that were consistent with the position he or she was taking.

Another means of testing the quality of a theory that has been generated from research findings in a primary research report is to test its empirical validity by determining how well the theory fits the findings of the various primary research reports. It is important to note that the goal of theory analysis is to identify the strengths, as well as the limitations, of specific theories. In challenging the applicability of some theories, meta-theory may also provide support for the relevance and utility of other theoretical options. In our research, we were able to compare and contrast theories of support in chronic illness with the findings of a wide range of studies related to support. We were then able to conclude that the task-specific model of support in chronic illness offers a considerably broader explanatory basis in this context than do theories such as the hierarchical-compensatory model of support.

ISSUES IN THEORY ANALYSIS

Sociologists have voiced criticism that meta-theory has led to a collection of unsubstantiated claims that fragment the collective understanding of the discipline. Although there has been much rebuttal to this criticism, the concern is well heeded. Because of the exploratory nature of meta-theory, the findings of meta-theory must always be regarded as open to speculation, not as an entirely satisfactory explanation of the nature and history of theory within the field of study. Such an analysis, however, will confirm the value of questioning theory within the body of research and the relevance of exploring the issues and concerns it raises. Meta-theory without accountability could be characterized as mere navel gazing and poor scholarship that contributes little to the understanding of the phenomenon of interest. As in all areas of research, meta-study researchers must aim for trustworthiness and accountability in their meta-theorizing.

As was illustrated in the examples provided in this chapter, meta-theory often results in questions about how theory has been interpreted and used by previous researchers. If researchers have devoted their careers to research that supports a specific theoretical frame, it is unlikely that they will welcome the findings of meta-study researchers who argue that this theory is inadequate or inappropriate to explain the phenomenon under study. Meta-study researchers must be fully aware that not all who learn of their conclusions will interpret them charitably, and so they must be prepared to back up their claims with incontestable data and decision trails. Although we have encouraged skepticism, questioning assumptions, and seeking alternative explanations as a useful strategy to focus one's gaze beyond the obvious interpretations, we recognize that drawing conclusions in direct contradiction with the tenets of established or accepted theorizing is not without some professional and personal risk. We also believe, however, that critical analysis of extant theories can serve as the impetus to lively scholarly debate. From our perspective, such debate ought to be considered healthy and productive, in that it creates the climate in which clarity becomes possible in considering the theoretical foundations of our understanding of human experience.

CONCLUSION

Meta-theory has been described in this chapter as a creative and systematic means of analyzing theory and its effects on research within a specific field of study. We have drawn on the example of the theory of stigma several times in this chapter because it clearly illustrates how meta-theory analysis can expose both the applications and the limitations of theories that otherwise appear clear and self-explanatory. Because stigma theory is so well established within the social and health science research literature, its utility in explaining human behavior and experience has rarely been questioned. Meta-theory has assisted us in expanding and clarifying many elements of this theory.

Despite its utility, meta-theory should be approached with some caution. For example, it is quite possible for meta-theorists to spark theoretical argument within a discipline without extending the outcomes of this process beyond the formation of a debating club (Zhao, 1996). As Zhao (1996) points out, debate for its own sake can contribute to "the quick end of the beginning of an otherwise promising movement" to extend and clarify the theoretical foundations of research in a field of study (p. 306). Meta-study researchers, therefore, must continually reflect on their motivations and work to contribute to the development of new understandings about the phenomena under study. They must work to build, and not only to tear down, in the theoretical domain.

Meta-theory is analogous to peeling away the layers of an onion. Each layer is revealed only when the previous layer is removed, yet the wise researcher understands that the current contribution will not be the final answer to the problem. Meta-theory raises our awareness about the context in which the theories we now hold have been created, developed, and institutionalized into our science. It helps us expand our understandings of why we think the way we do and what alternative ways of thinking might be possible if we shift our angle of vision only slightly. Further, meta-theory helps us understand that there are social, political, and philosophical implications to the theoretical claims we make, some that we may be able to appreciate and others that may only become apparent with the influence of time and space. From our experience, including meta-theoretical analysis within a meta-study project creates the conditions under which knowledge can be transformed into wisdom. Although we recognize this as perhaps the most complex and abstract of all meta-study processes, we also believe that it may ultimately produce the most comprehensive and important results.

7

META-SYNTHESIS

Each of the three analytic steps of meta-study—meta-data-analysis, meta-method, and meta-theory—provides a unique angle of vision from which to deconstruct and interpret a body of qualitatively derived knowledge about a particular phenomenon. Because the larger intent of the meta-study is not simply to raise questions about what is already known but also to build theoretical approaches that may extend what is currently possible, meta-synthesis represents the visionary and constructive outcome of an exhaustive analysis project. As has been explained in earlier chapters, it is well recognized that building more comprehensive, effective, elegant, and useful theoretical claims informed by a thorough analysis of the strengths and limitations of previous attempts has had a widespread appeal among qualitative researchers (Estabrooks et al., 1994; Jensen & Allen, 1996; Sandelowski et al., 1997; Sherwood, 1999). At the same time, however, the processes and procedures by which this may be attempted remain elusive.

In this chapter, we begin to consider meta-synthesis as it is shaped by the larger context of a meta-study project. The current thinking about meta-synthesis that is available in qualitative health research literature is limited almost entirely to the products of meta-data-analysis and typically ignores the crucial insights that can arise from both meta-method and meta-theory analyses. We advocate meta-synthesis because of the more comprehensive analytic foundation as an infinitely more thorough, transparent, and scholarly enterprise, and it is our intent in writing this book to stimulate increasingly sophisticated thinking in this direction. Like our colleagues who write in the field, we are daunted by the complexity of the process but also are excited by its promise.

THE PURPOSE

The appeal of meta-synthesis lies in our hunger for more true, more accurate, or more real explanations of phenomena and more coherent ways to make sense of them. To this point, we have been locating meta-study within the context of constructivist enterprises. In keeping with this context, we fully acknowledge that meta-synthesis is similarly a social construction. That said, however, we also believe that the purpose of engagement in meta-synthesis is not merely to add new ideas to the collection of available constructions. Rather, we are convinced that underlying the notion of social construction is a competing ideal of social responsibility, morality, and accountability. Nowhere is this truer than in the health sciences, where qualitative researchers have enthusiastically endorsed postmodern thinking to a point, but where they also stand firm on positions of ethics, the greater social good, and the socially mandated role of the professions. So, for example, although they may theoretically embrace a claim that pain is an entirely subjective experience, they never abandon the objective truths (referred to by Hammersley [1995] as "subtle realisms") they hold about predictable conditions under which persons can be expected to experience pain. The local anaesthetic is therefore applied to the jaw prior to a dental extraction regardless of any actual subjective pain experience, and despite a multiplicity of creative approaches to dental pain that appear from time to time, no one seriously considers the possibility of assuming that pain might not occur. Thus, even in the context of a knowledge base steeped in social construction, the health sciences researcher is always open to the possibility of a more plausible, coherent, complete, and useful construction of reality than is available from the currently popular understandings.

Similarly, although qualitative researchers often seek out and account for multiple truths and competing perspectives within the subjective world of health and illness, at some deeper level they are guided by a moral imperative toward a better quality of life and a more respectful and responsible health care system for all. Thus, the idea of a moderate realism, a shared and mutually agreed upon truth, lurks behind even the most relative and postmodern of qualitative health research projects (Angen, 2000; Crotty, 1998; Flew, 1991). We do qualitative research because we believe there may be answers to some of the larger questions we ask and because those answers may make a difference in how we theorize health and illness and how we practice our professions. Thus, meta-synthesis is driven, not by a frivolous urge to be creative about ideas or by a presumptuous desire to author a new way of understanding something, but by the abiding sense that the process may yield truths that are better, more socially relevant, or more complete than those from which we currently operate.

The object of a meta-synthesis, then, is not simply to report similarities within the research literature in relation to a particular phenomenon, or to account for common patterns within the available knowledge, or to reduce the available understandings to the lowest common denominator. Rather, it is to dig below the surface of what is currently understood, to draw on the most thorough analysis possible to deconstruct the validity of the ideas that are currently in favor, and to emerge with the kernel of a new truth, a better kind of understanding, or a more socially responsible form of theorizing something. In so doing, it creates the possibilities of looking beyond, imagining something better, and contributing to a more complex and infinitely interesting scholarship.

THE PROCEDURE

Meta-synthesis in the context of meta-study draws explicitly from each of the three prior processes and brings the insights they produce together to form theory in a new way. Because few researchers have considered meta-synthesis on this basis, there is little explicit procedural theory on which to draw. It is therefore much easier to caution the reader against challenges inherent in the process than to give explicit direction for how to accomplish meta-synthesis effectively. Our own experience working with these processes during several years in the context of a research team has led us to conclude that concretizing and codifying steps for meta-synthesis would probably reduce it to the more simplified processes that are easily described in the literature. Rather, we remain intrigued by the mystery and magic of how knowledge can be inductively derived through the full range of meta-study processes. So, we resist definitive procedural steps and encourage instead a dynamic and iterative process of thinking, interpreting, creating, theorizing, and reflecting. We do believe that, in domains like health and illness, all truths are not equally plausible or responsible and that the larger objective of seeking better and more effective ways of understanding complex human phenomena is an inherently worthwhile exercise. At the same time, we are quite comfortable with the idea that the struggle for understanding is perhaps far more important in the overall scheme of things than are the final answers. In our own work, we do not anticipate ever being able to create a complete and comprehensive theory of chronic illness experience that will surpass all others and effectively answer all questions in the field. We do believe, however, that we can create more effective ways of handling the conflicting knowledge that the field reflects. We can account for more variations within experience between people and across context and articulate linkages between ideas that reveal considerably more of their strengths and limitations than have previous attempts at theorizing. In so doing, we can challenge some of the currently available theories that systematically disadvantage certain people and situations, we can uncover some of the implications of taking on certain theoretical positionings, and we can urge our colleagues in the scholarly, as well as the clinical, communities to recognize the way their ideas and actions contribute to the context within which health and illness are experienced. On the basis of insights drawn from meta-data-analysis, meta-method, and meta-theory, we believe that it is possible to synthesize new knowledge that appreciably changes the way we work with the ideas that make up our various substantive worlds.

INSIGHTS FROM META-DATA-ANALYSIS

As has been discussed in earlier chapters, meta-data-analysis provides a technique of aggregating and making sense of findings from various individual pieces of research about a particular phenomenon. If its purpose is additive—in other words, simply reporting systematically that many studies of a thing reported similar findings—then the debate about methodological diversity becomes straightforward. It would clearly not be appropriate to add findings from one kind of study to those of another and expect to achieve an accurate summation of knowledge. When the meta-study approach to data is extended into a meta-synthesis, however, the inherent value of having access to findings deriving from a range of methodological and theoretical approaches becomes increasingly apparent.

Recognition of the explicit effects of methodological and theoretical variations on the findings that result from a particular kind of research provides a strategy by which data can be effectively decontextualized and interpreted. Thus, if we were to discover that grounded theory studies consistently found evidence of stages in anticipatory grieving, for example, we might have a strong foundation on which to understand distinct differences in the interpretation of the essence of grief experience—as depicted by different phenomenologies focusing on persons with different kinds of anticipatory grief contexts and at differing points within those experiences. Further, if our ethnographic studies of related phenomena were also added to the picture, the comprehensive portrait of anticipatory grieving might take on proportions that begin to account for human universals within the phenomenon, as well as for a range of possible variations. A synthesis of any one of these bodies of knowledge alone might erroneously assume truth only as it can be derived from a particular methodological orientation. Thus, although meta-data-analysis based on like methods makes sense, meta-synthesis using a narrow body of knowledge does not.

Our diabetes meta-study (Paterson et al., 1998) provided us with an opportunity to synthesize an interpretation of the various metaphorical representations (primarily of control and balance) inherent in the experience of living with this disease as they arose from the various contributions of a diverse body of qualitative studies. In examining contradictions and contrasts between the findings as a starting point, we began to speculate about what they meant and to generate possible hypotheses that would explain their variations. For example, people who assume active participation in decisions about their diabetes often perceive their experience with diabetes as balanced. Social construction of acceptance of diabetes has been commonly associated with living as normally as possible, and this leads to a perception of balance in living with diabetes. As researchers, we asked questions of the data, particularly how the historical and sociocultural contexts influenced the research findings. In so doing, we discovered that several researchers in studies involving participants of nondominant ethnicity often concluded that understanding illness in a personally relevant and meaningful way is essential to balance. We wondered whether this finding reflected assumptions about health beliefs that were culturally determined or whether it was an artifact of how the researchers phrased the question. We asked ourselves whether dominant (Caucasian) participants would be asked about their beliefs in the same manner and, if not, why not?

Using the hypothetical path analysis strategy as described by Miles and Huberman (1994) for comparisons across cases, we diagrammed our hypotheses that participation in decision making, use of a glucometer, type of diabetes, and duration of diabetes might bear some relationship to this notion of balance. We then returned to the primary research data to determine whether they supported a schematic representation of how balance was attained in living with diabetes. We discovered that some aspects of our diagram had weak or contradictory evidential support in the data. For example, although most primary researchers pointed to the role of active involvement in decision making as promoting balance in living with diabetes, others indicated that the participants in their research who were unwilling or unable to assume such a role still experienced balance. This discovery caused us to explore further the meaning of assuming an active role in decision making and to ask why some people do not need to assume such a role to achieve balance. We were thus led to the finding that balance is achieved by assuming an active role in decision making only if the individual values and is able to assume such a role; in contrast, when individuals consider active participation in decision making to be low in priority, beyond their abilities, or inappropriate, efforts by health care professionals to foster such active involvement can actually create imbalance and endanger health. Although this synthesis may not have represented a comprehensive new understanding of the field, it did extend the available knowledge in a manner that might assist clinicians and theoreticians in reconciling the variations within the research reports and in making more effective decisions about the use of overarching metaphoric representations related to balance and control.

Beyond meta-data-analysis, meta-synthesis can take the researcher into the domain of the assumptions underlying a body of research findings and the interpretations that have been made about it. In particular, it can extend the interpretation from what has been studied to what has not and can permit speculation about why this might be so. Although meta-data-analysis is a useful exercise in its own right, we believe that the process of trying to work with both aggregations and contradictions arising from qualitative data is integral to a truly exciting and illuminating meta-synthesis. When new interpretations are presented in the context of the old and elucidate relationships between the various discrete components of the old, they can be said to truly extend knowledge in the field.

INSIGHTS FROM META-METHOD

Meta-method offers a strategy by which to reflect on the role of methodological orientation and decision making as it shapes the findings of individual studies, and it also provides an angle from which to interpret a body of knowledge as it has evolved. From meta-method analysis, we begin (a) to identify the nuances in the various qualitative approaches that have been applied and the patterns in how and why such approaches may have been used in contrast with others and (b) to consider in a more abstract sense the kinds of knowledge that may not have been included in currently held conceptualizations as a result of these methodological choices. To some extent, method reflects academic discipline, in that certain disciplines have long been associated with the development and ownership of certain methodological traditions, but to an extensive degree, the original role of disciplinary orientation has been blurred as qualitative health researchers have adopted, adapted, and refined their approaches to answering research questions (Thorne, 1991). Therefore, the method, even more than the theoretical or disciplinary orientation, can often account for what we think we know about a field through analysis of the available body of qualitative research reports.

Although analytic methods in qualitative research have certain common practices (e.g., establishing codes to represent data), each analytic approach carries specific assumptions about the nature of the data, the relationship of the researcher to the data, and the way analyzed data should be represented. Data analysis in the realm of social interactionism, for example, is founded on an assumption that the interpretation of the meaning of a phenomenon is derived in interaction between group members and between researcher and participants (Miles & Huberman, 1994). In contrast, the analytic processes of critical social research are based on the assumption that the taken-for-granted and the invisible can produce oppressive structures. These assumptions shape the nature of the data that are collected and the way they are analyzed. Social inter-actionism research, for example, aims at condensing the data to define the way a particular group views and gives meaning to the phenomenon under study. Critical social researchers, however, strive to "unpack" the meaning a particular group attributes to the phenomenon and thereby to discover the hidden and taken-for-granted.

The process of exploring and analyzing the impact of assumptions underlying data analysis requires a fairly intimate familiarity with the epistemological and ontological foundations of many approaches to data analysis. In the meta-synthesis phase of a meta-study, the intent is not to judge the relative merits of the various analytic options, but rather to try to appreciate how they may have influenced the nature of the research findings. For example, whereas some analytic methods capitalize on capturing and accounting for intricate variations within original data, others focus on collapsing variations into an increasingly smaller number of researcher-identified codes and categories. In some cases, this kind of process disembodies the data from the person who produced them and the context in which they were derived (Conrad, 1990). Thus, meta-method allows the meta-synthesist to consider the degree to which the context and language of the primary research participants may have been sacrificed to expedite categorizing the data and whether this may have implications for the body of knowledge that has ensued.

Meta-method thereby offers an angle of vision from which broader understandings of phenomena can be synthesized. For example, if we can determine from an examination of qualitative research that family caregivers of older adults with dementia camouflage their feelings of anger with health care professionals, then we can begin to make sense of why various kinds of researchers—asking various kinds of questions, representing various health professional disciplines, and interpreting data according to various methodological traditions—can produce conclusions that may dramatically over- or underrepresent the manifestations of anger that are most common in this situation. Understanding the impact of such factors as the age or ethnicity of the cohort, the sociocultural proscriptions against overt expressions of anger, and the risks that might be associated with professional concern about one's caregiving quality provides a context in which a more refined and comprehensive understanding of the caregiving experience might be possible. By comparing studies that used retrospective accounts (in which caregivers may have made peace with their limitations in the role or may have reframed the situation as a necessary sacrifice), or studies that used participant observation (in which various masks may have been employed to reduce access to deeper or unpleasant emotional material), with studies that relied on intensive interviewing during the caregiving period (in which the material that might be reported would be only that to which the caregiver allowed him- or herself conscious access), a better theoretical construction of the phenomenon, accounting for all these predictable features, becomes possible. Thus, meta-method contributes to a meta-synthesis in creating the framework within which different discoveries about a phenomenon can be understood and contextualized.

INSIGHTS FROM META-THEORY

Meta-theory creates the context in which the implications of a range of theoretical approaches that have influenced the body of knowledge can be considered and evaluated. In addition, new theoretical alternatives that might account for a more comprehensive, accurate, or credible interpretation of the phenomenon can be synthesized. As has been discussed in earlier chapters, each primary study can be best understood when it is considered in its demographic, theoretical, and historic context. This step allows the researcher to understand in a different way why primary researchers may have obtained different findings at different times.

The overt or covert theoretical underpinnings of every piece of qualitative research contribute powerfully to the findings generated and the interpretations made on the basis of those findings. Although meta-theory allows us to extract the findings from their theoretical infrastructure, it also provides a foundation on which alternative theoretical understandings can be tested and considered. In some cases, this meta- analytic process leads to the conclusion that the research was not about the substantive focus it purported to be (e.g., the concept, the clinical phenomenon, or the health challenge it addressed) but was actually designed as a means to develop, expand, or strengthen a predetermined theoretical position. For example, if a body of research is driven by a theoretical claim about the applications of certain kinds of cognitions, and if the various studies seek to articulate those cognitions in a collection of different clinical contexts, then the meta-theory process will help the analyst confidently conclude that the cognitive features of the various diseases or conditions are relevant only if one assumes a specific theoretical position. Similarly, if the conclusions of a particular study are articulated in such a manner that they confirm the relevance of the theory by which the study was guided (what Johnson [1999] referred to as "uncritical verificationism"), the meta-synthesist may conclude that this body of research might yield insight for a meta-synthesis of the *theoretical position* but not for a meta-synthesis of the *clinical condition* on which the theory was tested. Thus, meta-theory creates a way of thinking about the theoretical underpinnings of ideas that not only exposes the implications of certain kinds of theoretical frames applicable in qualitative research but also generates standards by which the conclusions of certain pieces of research can be, more or less, heavily credited with creating useful and applicable knowledge.

By interpreting both the methodological and theoretical contexts within which various findings have been generated, the meta-synthesist creates a sound theoretical basis for determining which among the existing findings are most relevant to a newly synthesized theory and which may be respectfully ignored or discarded. This step can be extremely helpful in determining why the observable differences in findings occur and then comfortably concluding how to interpret those differences. The contrast between the findings of research conducted by Carpenter (1994) and Laskiwiski (1990a, 1990b; Laskiwiski & Morse 1993) on coping with spinal cord injury is a case in point. Carpenter studied the experience of spinal-cord-injured persons who lived in the community, whereas Laskiwiski investigated the experience of more recently injured individuals in a hospital rehabilitation unit. Although both researchers studied the same phenomenon, their choice of contexts and the differences in the duration of disability within their samples resulted in vastly different ways of describing the experience of living with a spinal cord injury. Laskiwiski noted the way spinal-cord-injured patients use such strategies as jokes and swearing to cope with the implications of their injury and to develop a sense of community with other clients on the unit.

Carpenter, in contrast, noted the important impact on individuals with spinal cord injuries of support from others, self-identity, and self-management in being able to cope with community living. It seems probable that their distinct disciplinary perspectives (Carpenter being a rehabilitation scientist, and Laskiwiski being a nurse) created predictable differences in the kinds of questions they thought worthy of study, the way they focused their gaze within the clinical context, and the sense they made of the various contextual issues that emerged as they generated their findings. These disciplinary and theoretical frames may well explain why Carpenter may not have attended to the meaning of joking and swearing, if indeed she detected it in the individuals within her sample, and why Laskiwiski may not have contemplated community structural supports if her priority was to observe interpersonal and identity issues in the immediate aftermath of devastating injury. In this instance, although the reported findings of these two studies are considerably different, the differences are entirely understandable in the context of the theoretical and methodological positions within which the two pieces of research were grounded. In the context of these theoretical underpinnings, we would interpret no particular conflict between the two studies and indeed would appreciate that they both might be quite usefully applied to synthesize a more comprehensive theory about how persons with spinal cord injuries adapt to and manage their disability over time.

SYNTHESIZING INSIGHTS

When insights from meta-data-analysis, meta-method, and meta-theory are brought together, the meta-study researcher will typically encounter many more questions than answers. Although a synthesis of knowledge seems quite plausible on the basis of studies using similar samples, similar methods, and similar theoretical understandings, we have argued quite strongly in this discussion that this type of synthesis generally represents mere aggregation. In aggregating findings of like inquiries, we are not really provided any more confidence in our conclusions or better understandings of a phenomenon; instead, we learn that if we ask questions in a particular way, we will get a predictable set of answers. In contrast, meta-synthesis capitalizes on diversity of context, method, and theoretical orientation to allow the possibility of a richer, deeper, and more multifaceted way of theorizing about a phenomenon.

As we begin to account for more layers of the thing we are studying, as we consider it from an increasingly diverse number of angles, and as we challenge it with more and more theoretical interpretations, we create the possibility of coming closer and closer to appreciating an essential nature, or an inherent reality.

Even though many modern philosophers within our midst would immediately discount the possibility of ever knowing the true essence of a thing, we in health care share a passionate commitment to trying. Pain may or may not exist as an objective reality independent of our social constructions about it, but the role of the clinician or clinical researcher in the pain clinic is to get closer to a true understanding of what pain is, how we can make sense of it, how we can ameliorate it, and how we can support those who must experience it. Each of these issues represents a reality around which we can envision improvements in our theorizing, more effective understandings, and a higher quality of knowledge application. Meta-synthesis therefore requires a leap of faith that knowledge can progress toward more comprehensive, specific, or useful theorizing than currently available to us and that some of the theorizing may derive from the knowledge acquired through qualitative research.

PRODUCTS OF META-SYNTHESIS

In most meta-study projects, it will not be possible to predict the degree to which new theory can be synthesized until the products of meta-data-analysis, meta-method, and meta-theory are individually and collectively interpreted. Typically, as we have observed in all our meta-study projects, the process inspires more pessimism than optimism because of the gaps, flaws, and limitations it can reveal within a body of qualitative inquiry. It must be recognized that this rigorous analytic process involves an extended critical deconstruction of what is known and how it is known, and many analysts will find it difficult to get past the conclusion that "we know nothing!" In our consultations with others who have ventured into this territory, we understand that despair about truth and knowledge is a frequent experience and can become an insecure foundation on which to try to generate new theorizing.

We do believe, however, that the key to a successful meta-synthesis effort lies in recognizing that small gains can be as important as larger ones and that better ways of theorizing about narrow aspects of a field may be more useful in the long run than are completely original grand theories. In our chronic illness meta-study project, for example, we came to realize that our dream of creating a comprehensive new way of theorizing chronic illness was remarkably naive. At the same time, however, we discovered several current claims in relation to chronic illness whose contradictions could be reconciled and whose theoretical applications could be extended. In that context, for example, we applied our insights about historical trends in the interpretation of data to a recognition that "opposites," such as loss and gain, burden and opportunity, could coexist within every chronic illness experience and be brought to the foreground in varying degrees, depending on the purpose of the interaction, the current context, the intensity of adaptation required, and the sociocultural values inherent in any individual situation (Thorne & Paterson, 1998). In addition, we were able to synthesize a new theory of transformation in chronic illness that challenged the assumptions of previous theorists in the field, reconciled the rather dramatically different values these theorists represented, and reduced the oversimplification that many of them fell prey to in characterizing a "good life" with a chronic disease (Paterson et al., 1999). We proposed that transformation be understood as a cognitive and affective means of mediating the effects of a chronic illness. As such, transformation reflects nothing more than a personal choice, and not an ethereal reward for having lived successfully with the disease. Although these may seem like minor theoretical accomplishments in the larger scheme of things, we are satisfied that they represent something larger than our individual pieces of research could possibly attain. We believe that meta-study has given us a much more comprehensive and complete way of understanding the field, of putting research products in context, and of imagining the truly magnificent kinds of theorizing that may become possible in the future.

CONCLUSION

In this chapter, we considered the way the analytic processes of meta-data-analysis, meta-method, and meta-theory each bring an angle of vision to a body of qualitative research, laying the groundwork for meta-synthesis of new knowledge. In contrast with mere analysis, in which the parts are distinguished and critically examined, or aggregation, in which the conclusions are summarily condensed into a confident claim, meta-synthesis takes the insights developed to a new level of awareness and creates the possibility of stronger, more complete, or more theoretically responsible ways of understanding or interpretation.

In the domain of health research, meta-synthesis creates a strategy from which the artifacts of theorizing, methodology, and data grounding can be extracted from the substantive conclusions of a generation of studies, and the possibility of more real realities, or truer truths, emerges. Even though theorizing for its own sake has no moral agenda, we in the health domain are vigilant for an array of implications that derive from the ideas we hold. Which ideas we will use to guide our practices and our policies, and which ideas we will reject as impossible, unsafe, impractical, or socially irresponsible will be a product of the interaction between excellent theorizing and deep convictions about truth. Meta-study offers us a path to follow in developing wisdom about the field of study in which we are engaged, in making effective decisions about the theoretical directions we wish to pursue, and in reconciling a world of multiple and coexisting realities with those doctrines we hold incontestable. From time to time, it may also place us in a position of sufficient clarity, strength, and understanding that we can truly synthesize new knowledge.

8

EVALUATION, DISSEMINATION, AND FUTURE CHALLENGES

The processes of meta-study have been described and explained in the preceding chapters. It should by now be clear that this research approach, grounded in a constructivist perspective, extends beyond traditional processes of analysis and synthesis into a domain consolidating theoretical perspectives, methods, and findings into new ways of theorizing. Just as explication of process is essential to understanding research, so is a discussion of the evaluation and dissemination of meta-study findings. Exploration of these aspects of meta-study completes the picture and provides a lens through which to consider the future evolution of this genre of research.

EVALUATION OF META-STUDY OUTCOMES

Because of the exploratory and often speculative nature of meta-study, researchers applying it should subscribe to rigorous standards of quality. The findings of meta-study research will be scrutinized and eventually accepted or rejected on the basis of standards implied by the complexity and comprehensiveness of the method. Further, the research will be understood and evaluated primarily in relation to its significance for understanding the field. Meta-study that is technically correct but meaningless to researchers will not find acceptance within the scholarly community.

A significant measure of the quality of a meta-study is that it should provide a credible and comprehensive answer to the research question(s) through logically developed conclusions (Cooper, 1986). The purpose of the meta-study should be explicit, the theoretical framework directing the sampling should serve as a basis for the interpretation of the findings, the inclusion/exclusion criteria used in the selection of primary research reports should be identified, and sufficient detail should be provided to enable replication of the meta-study.

As with all research, meta-studies are evaluated on their adherence to general guidelines and principles of design. Thus, it is important to articulate the bases on which inclusion and exclusion criteria were determined; the scope, range, and nature of the data gathering procedures; and the nature of the eventual sample of primary studies on which the meta-study was based. The logic of decision-making processes in relation to all design steps should be transparent and auditable. Because so many of the interpretations and conclusions in meta-data-analysis, meta-method, and meta-theory are based on tentative ideas—theoretical hunches, digging below the surface to test wild hypotheses, and brainstorming as many alternative explanations as possible—failure to explicate the reasoning processes from which the ultimate conclusions are drawn will detract significantly from the credibility of the work. Because the focus of the critical analysis will be on the methodological, theoretical, or contextual biases that the primary researchers may have held and that may have influenced their findings, it is especially important for the meta-study researcher to strive for as much objective neutrality as possible and to account for the logic by which conclusions were reached in both the analysis and the synthesis phases.

Techniques for making the meta-study reasoning processes transparent and auditable include explicit clarification and resolution of differences and contradictions among the primary research reports, including alternative explanations that might have been possible and the rationale for the one that has been determined. Thus, both the predominant views and the outlier perspectives should be apparent in the meta-study report.

In so doing, the meta-study researcher reveals a high degree of openness and reflexivity (Zhao, 1991). Researcher reflexivity can also be explicit through the inclusion of speculation about possible reasons for the meta-study findings, using a variety of theories and perspectives as a foundation for this discussion.

Another measure of the quality of a meta-study is how it nests; that is, a study of high quality will demonstrate careful examination of each primary research report individually and will reveal the degree to which it is embedded in the body of research, the sociocultural and political contexts, and the researcher's disciplinary and theoretical traditions (Ritzer, 1992b). The collection of primary research reports should therefore tell a story about the body of knowledge that reveals how strands of inquiry have built upon one another, how disparate directions in research may have developed concurrently, or how dominant theorists influenced the way the phenomenon has been studied and understood over time. As has been noted by others, it can be difficult to maintain the integrity of the individual primary research studies while avoiding the problem of so much detail that "no usable synthesis is produced" (Sandelowski, 1997, p. 130). Thus, a high-quality meta-synthesis will do justice to the body of primary research in a manner that provides sufficient information for the reader to track sources and decisions, but it will focus the majority of the discussion on the products of meta-data-analysis, meta-method, and meta-theory.

Beyond procedural evaluation, judging the quality of a meta-study project involves consideration of four essential questions:

1. Has it increased our understanding of the body of research in the field of study?
2. Has it illuminated the implications of the contexts, methods, and theories that have influenced the body of research in the field?
3. Has it generated new or expanded theory?
4. Has it articulated an alternative overarching perspective about the phenomenon?

If a meta-study has not produced new theorizing, it will be important to determine whether the research team has simply exhausted its enthusiasm for the subject or has quite correctly concluded that such theorizing would be premature or incongruous, given the current status of knowledge.

If a new theoretical meta-synthesis has been articulated, its relationship to the existing field and its consistency with the meta-data-analysis, meta-method, and meta-theory conclusions must be self-evident. Finally, if it is to be convincing, especially to an audience invested in one or another of the theoretical positions that it challenges, it must be consistent, parsimonious, and elegant (Cooper & Lindsay, 1998, p. 333).

DISSEMINATION OF META-STUDY FINDINGS

The dissemination of meta-study research findings can be complicated by two distinct aspects of meta-study research: (a) The sampled primary research reports represent a discrete timeline, and (b) the range of options for the potential audiences to be considered in the dissemination process may be infinite. The currency of the primary research data set becomes a concern because, in any meta-study project, the publication of new research studies and ideas about research will occur concurrently with the meta-analysis and meta-synthesis. Although an exhaustive research process is wise, it can become problematic if the claims and conclusions seem to relate to "yesterday's news" and fail to account for the developments that have been published in the meantime. Although the historical retrospective may be informative, potential audiences may discount its usefulness if subsequent research seems to have corrected the problems identified or to have filled in any gaps noted. Thus, a time pressure is on the meta-study researcher if the product of the work is to provide new or elaborated understandings of the phenomenon under study.

As with all scholars, meta-study researchers are under pressure to publish and present what they have discovered in the meta-study in a timely manner so that they might guide other researchers toward productive and appropriate directions before general understanding of the phenomenon of interest changes significantly with time. Although it is usually not possible to integrate new primary research reports into a meta-project once it is well underway, meta-study researchers must remain aware of the current research so that their claims about the field retain relevance. Thus, it may be prudent to distinguish in the write-up of meta-study results those primary studies that have been included in the data analysis, as well as those that may have appeared subsequently and have only been considered in the context of discussing the study's implications.

Another issue relating to the dissemination of findings is the multiplicity of subsidiary or future projects that may emanate from a large meta-study. For example, in our chronic illness meta-study, it would have been possible to conduct discrete meta-study interpretations of any of the 22 distinct diseases that are the focus of the primary research reports. Meta-study could also have been conducted on any of the major concepts arising from the chronic illness experience research (e.g., courage, stigma, normalization, quality of life) or on any of the processes implied in the research conclusions (e.g., adaptation, trajectory of illness, coping). Thus, accountability for the overall project must involve thoughtful and defensible decisions about which ideas are inherent aspects of the meta-study itself and which might be considered secondary or subsequent analytic enterprises. We discovered, for example, that because of the number of discrete diseases and concepts in our chronic illness meta-study, team members working on various pieces easily lost track of who else was working on what. Also, once individual team members followed the threads of logic that each challenge posed, they sometimes found themselves heading into territory that overlapped with that of other members of the team.

Because the credibility of a meta-study project demands that each individual researcher and each group of researchers drawing from the meta-study convey compatible analyses and insights (at least to some extent), a system must be in place to monitor all presentation and publication activities. This monitoring function may feel contrary to what many independent researchers are accustomed to doing, and therefore such a process requires vigilance. In our chronic illness project, for example, we found it difficult to allow for a full team review of all claims if individual members were in a last-minute rush to meet submission or conference deadlines. Thus, some of our individual working habits did require modification or fine tuning. For this reason, it may be helpful to have a designated leader for the team or some explicit process that allows all team members to remain fully aware of each theme within the work as it evolves. Ideally, regular team meetings at which full reports of what work is being done or contemplated are shared and full disclosure of all manuscript and presentation drafts should be considered an integral part of the meta-study design. In a complex enterprise such as a meta-study project, prior agreement about such issues as authorship and ongoing mechanisms to ensure clear and effective communication is particularly important. In an ideal world, all team members consistently follow through with all commitments and contribute equally to the project's success. In the real world, such issues often require serious and difficult negotiations and, if not effectively resolved, may derail a team effort.

A final issue that arises regarding the dissemination of meta-study results is the matter of determining the most appropriate audiences for dissemination efforts and how best to ensure these audiences appropriate access to the findings. For example, some findings of our chronic illness meta-study have applications in social and health policy at a provincial or national governmental level. The traditional routes of publishing in refereed academic journals and of presenting at scholarly conferences will typically have no impact whatsoever on the thinking of government officials. As we know, findings of qualitative research in general are not even disseminated beyond the researcher's own discipline (Patton, 1990). In our opinion, therefore, meta-study researchers have a solemn obligation to develop creative strategies for marketing the findings to specific audiences beyond traditional academic routes of dissemination and beyond the narrow confines of their own particular disciplinary orientation.

Potential audiences of meta-study findings include all who may hold some stake in the implications of the research. These groups may be numerous and varied and can span several populations, including specific client groups and researchers interested in a particular theory or concept. To identify potential stakeholders in meta-study research and what information they might require, you might ask the following questions:

- Who might be interested in the information?
- What is the nature of their interest?
- How will they use the information?
- What is the most appropriate vehicle for disseminating the information to them?
- How can the findings be appropriately contextualized?

Often, representatives of a stakeholder group can be an excellent source of answers to these questions, helping you make effective dissemination decisions.

One audience often overlooked in disseminating research is the public at large. We were reminded of this recently by a group of research participants in another study who insisted that we "get out there in the public" with our findings. When asked about the forum that would best accomplish that goal, they agreed that popular magazines, local cable television programs, and radio interviews would be excellent venues for disseminating the findings of our research. Because our academic training typically orients us toward academic vehicles for research dissemination, many of us did not even consider the potential impact we might have with more creative and accessible strategies.

Given the complexity and investment a meta-study requires, we believe that dissemination of findings is of critical importance. Not only does it facilitate a dialogue with participant groups, other stakeholders, and policymakers, but it also creates opportunities to expand the analysis and to network with other theorists and researchers. As the ideas that can be stimulated in a meta-study project filter into the thinking of a range of scholars, there is potential for a serious challenge to the status quo in theory and research within the field.

CHALLENGING TRADITIONAL PRACTICES

As the impetus for meta-study research is often found in issues within a field of study (Zhao, 1991), it is not surprising that those with an investment in the way research has been conducted in the past may view meta-study results with some degree of defensiveness. Thus, unless their findings are disseminated with some sensitivity, meta-study researchers run the risk of being perceived as tearing down the body of knowledge rather than as contributing to its development.

Meta-study leads researchers to understand what has been "ignored, misconstrued, or mistreated" (Kasper, 1994, p. 268) within a field of study. It can be tempting to concentrate primarily on what has gone wrong or what is missing from previous research rather than on what the research may have contributed to an understanding of the phenomenon. This may represent a particularly challenging trap for meta-study researchers who enter a project with an agenda to correct perceived errors within the existing body of knowledge. Thus, a hallmark of accomplished research will include being able to comment thoughtfully on the strengths, as well as the limitations, within a body of knowledge. Keep in mind that no body of scholarship has evolved without some areas of ambiguity and that all understandings of phenomena will evolve as researchers learn from one another's mistakes, as well as triumphs. What was judicious research at an earlier time within a field of study may have become ill-advised simply because knowledge in the area has increased and there are new and greater demands for alternative approaches and theoretical frameworks (Messeri, Silverstein, & Litwak, 1993).

A danger with presenting meta-study findings as "a new enlightenment" is the resultant tendency to "throw the baby out with the bath water." For example, although many data arising from our chronic illness meta-study support a critique of the concept of compliance in chronic illness research, it would be inappropriate to suggest that reference to the notion of compliance presumes counterproductive power relations between patients and health care providers. By challenging that body of research as indicative of hegemonic understanding, we could miss the alternative notion that patients may want, at times, to understand their own behaviors as noncompliant. Thus, replacing overly simplistic theorizing with alternative theories at a similar level of complexity and abstraction may complicate rather than resolve theoretical problems. Although the process of meta-study can sensitize the research team to many crucial issues within the research, it cannot guarantee that their own newly synthesized interpretations will themselves be beyond reproach.

In our chronic illness meta-study project, we became so excited initially about the insights we derived from the process that we became rather like prophets without constraint; we presented the future imperatives for research in the area so passionately that we unintentionally conveyed that much of what researchers had done to date had been misguided. This did little to endear us to our colleagues who had worked so diligently to uncover understandings in the field of chronic illness research. We are now learning to present our findings as the next step, building on the individual questions, theoretical perspectives, and methods that formed the foundation for such a work. When presenting the insights we have gained from the meta-study, we do not hesitate to present findings that are in conflict with the way researchers have viewed chronic illness in the past. The difference, however, is that we now stay consciously aware of our audience, knowing that it is not a mark of academic scholarship to dismiss summarily all that has come before in the field of study!

FUTURE DIRECTIONS

In the preceding chapters, we presented the structure and processes of meta-study, a qualitative research aggregation approach. Meta-study is a systematic study of a body of qualitative research in which the interactions among theory, research findings, and research methods are like those of dancers in a ballet, each contributing uniquely, yet together, to the rhythm, interpretation, and essence of the dance. The four components of meta-study—meta-data-analysis, meta-method, meta-theory, and meta-synthesis—are entwined to produce new or expanded understanding of a body of qualitative research, revealing future possibilities for the development of theoretical as well as practice knowledge.

Harding (1987) proposed that there are essentially three forms of data collection in qualitative research: (a) listening to informants, (b) observing behavior, and (c) examining documents or materials such as photographs. Meta-study is yet another form. It moves beyond methods that investigate individual subjectivity to actively transform our understanding of human behavior and experience. It is oriented toward the clarification of contentious issues, resolving arguments and debates and allowing for greater synthesis and integration within a particular field of study (Ritzer, 1992b).

Meta-study is also an example of what McKinlay (1979) terms "upstream endeavors" (p. 9), in which researchers attempt to address economic, political, or social factors that shape the experience of health and illness by extending the microperspective of research (individual-based research) to a macroscopic or social change perspective. Although we need both perspectives in nursing and health care (Butterfield, 1990; Cummings, 1987), there is a danger that if we continue to focus on individual-based research, we will be left without the understanding or tools needed to address the complex social, political, and economic forces shaping the behavior and experience of populations.

Zhao (1991) proposes that meta-study is a product of a time in which there is a crisis about what has been done and what needs to be done in the future to advance a discipline. Qualitative "insider" research has indeed reached such a point of crisis. An array of qualitative studies offer individual accounts of experience, but it is difficult to discern their collective significance for the future of practice, research, or education in any discipline. Meta-study offers an examination of changes and problems that have occurred within a field of study and the possibility of revising the "travel plans, or even having second thoughts on the final destination" (Zhao, 1991, p. 81).

Meta-study research has been challenged as being nothing more than a critique of work by other researchers, too vague to be of practical use (Ritzer, 1992b). Insufficient legitimation of meta-study research contributes to this view, and skepticism about the method is likely to continue until there is enough credible meta-study research to counteract these criticisms. Critics are uncertain about what they are attacking, and meta-study researchers lack confidence about what they are defending because the method has not yet been sufficiently tested or evolved. In the meantime, it is imperative that meta-study researchers clarify the procedures and standards they use.

The use of meta-study, as we have adapted it from its sociological origins to synthesize qualitative health research, is in its infancy. We believe that we have addressed the limitations of previous efforts to synthesize qualitative research, such as vague terms and procedures, by detailing the steps and rationale for the processes we have developed during several meta-study projects. Although we would not advocate meta-study as an appropriate strategy for all researchers or for all bodies of research, we see considerable excitement within the qualitative health research community for better guidance and support for such approaches.

We expect a bright future for meta-study research in the qualitative health field. Many research questions will force investigators farther than the scope of specific qualitative research endeavors and into analysis and synthesis of what is known beyond the reach of our individual theoretical samples. Indeed, as our examples have illustrated, the components of meta-study have been practiced at least covertly by many researchers to date. As they are applied in research, the processes of meta-study will become refined and expanded by the researchers who employ them. We eagerly await the challenges and contributions of our colleagues in this regard.

The coming of age of meta-study within qualitative health research means the time has come for researchers to pursue "fresh hints, for explorations of new intuitions which may reach beyond old conclusions, set categories, and conventional methods" (Brueggermann, 1977, p. xi). The capacity to interpret existing bodies of qualitative research by using meta-study will permit researchers to argue for substantive and meaningful revisions in the ways we have conducted our research and interpreted phenomena to this point in our collective history. The expanded scope of meta-study allows us to address new issues arising from our inquiries, to articulate new theories about phenomena that intrigue us, and to challenge the dominant intellectual traditions that have shaped our disciplinary understandings to this juncture. As we become increasingly sophisticated in our analysis of how the various bodies of qualitative research have evolved, we will gain credibility in our efforts to convince practitioners, funding agencies, governments, and policymakers that the outcomes of qualitative research can and must influence health policy and practice (McKinlay, 1992; O'Neill & Pederson, 1992). Using synthesis strategies such as those made possible by meta-study, we can transform the accumulated findings of a generation of qualitative researchers in nursing and health care from a collection of small studies into a legitimate body of knowledge. In so doing, we can extend the power of qualitative research to make a genuine difference to health care practitioners, policymakers, and clients.

Our experience using meta-study has indeed convinced us that such work is exciting, intellectually challenging, and ultimately constructive for a common purpose. We believe that extending existing competencies into these complex methodological strategies for answering research questions requires considerable commitment, courage, and openness on the part of those who engage in this process. Although such research approaches are in their infancy in the social and health sciences, we hope that sharing our own thoughts and experiences with readers will help smooth the path for increasing levels of excellence in this type of academic enterprise. We extend the challenge and invite you to join us in this endeavor.

Appendix A:

Primary Research Appraisal Tool

Code: 001

Reference: Paterson, B., & Sloan, J. (1994). A phenomenological study of the decision-making experience of individuals with long-standing diabetes. *Canadian Journal of Diabetes Care, 18*(4), 10-19.

Chronic Disease(s): Type I diabetes

Major Construct/Theory Investigated (if applicable): Self-care decision making

Genre of Study (e.g., grounded theory, phenomenology, narrative analysis): Interpretive phenomenology

(*Note: If stated genre does not appear to match the research design, elaborate on the lack of fit.):

Nature of Sample:

Total Number: 9

Ages: Not stated   Mean ages: N/A

Number of men:1   Number of women: 8

Ethnicity of sample: Caucasian

Education of sample: Not stated

Other characteristics:

- Nominated by diabetes internist or educator as successful in self-care management
- Two or more diabetes-related complications

General Description of Research Approach:

- One semistructured interview (2 hours long) based on participant's story (paradigm case) of experience in making a decision re self-care management
- A pilot study for larger research project

Major Findings:

1. Deciding to Assume Control Is the First Step in Learning to Make Independent Self-care Decisions.

- deciding to take charge of self-care management decisions

- growing up as a diabetic—process similar to developmental growth; there is an infancy, adolescence, and adulthood

2. Assuming Control Entails the Following:

- knowing the body = the key to personal control. Being able to interpret body's responses to interventions/situations. Reading the body. Have to know the basics of disease management first. Learning one's own patterns. Blood glucose readings = means of controlling the disease, not something that controls you.

- anticipating problems = when threats to control may occur. Hospitalization, with being treated as a textbook case and protocols, a major threat. When health care professional does not listen or understand about unique body responses. No two diabetics are alike.

- establishing collaborative relationships = partnership with health care professional in which each acknowledges the expertise of the other. Neither has all the answers. Communication in open and connected way. Knowing each other critical to forming this type of relationship. Knowing is respecting credibility and trustworthiness of the other. Depends on willingness of health care professional to listen to what the person has to say and to consider this in plan of care.

- fostering support = reading about the disease, joining support groups, learning from more experienced diabetics about establishing collaborative relationships, learning to ask for and accept support from others.

Research Design:

a. Problem Statement

- Statement of the phenomenon leads directly to the purpose of the study and the research question? Yes [✔] No [ ]

b. Purpose of the Research
- clearly expressed? Yes [✔] No [ ]
- significance of research problem clearly indicated? Yes [✔] No [ ]

c. Research Questions
- explicitly expressed? Yes [✔] No [ ]

- evidence of flow from the phenomenon? Yes [✔] No [ ]

d. Identification of Assumptions
  - identification of assumptions, preconceptions, presuppositions of researcher? Yes [✔] No [ ]   Not Applicable [ ]

e. Identification of Theoretical Framework
  - identification of theoretical framework? Yes [ ] No [✔]
  - if "yes," name framework (if it is not well-known, include a description):
  - clarification of influence of theoretical framework? Yes [ ]   No [ ]   Not Applicable [✔]

f. Researcher Credentials
  - documentation of researcher's discipline? Yes [✔] No [ ]
  - if "yes," name it: Nursing
  - any other pertinent information about the researcher (e.g., methodological preference, conceptual preference)?: Sloan is a statistician.
  - name(s) of persons acknowledged by the author(s): None

g. Role of Researcher
  - nonresearch relationship of researcher to participants (e.g., staff member of hospital, no previous relationship, unknown): No previous relationship
  - evidence that researcher has considered the effect of his/her presence on the research findings? Yes [ ] No [✔]
  - evidence that researcher has considered possibility of researcher bias or misinterpretation? Yes [✔] No [ ]

h. Sampling and Participants
  - description of type of sampling procedure? Yes [✔] No [ ]
  - identification of inclusion criteria? Yes [✔] No [ ]
  - discussion of attrition in longitudinal studies? Yes [ ] No [ ] Not Applicable [✔]

i. Data Gathering Strategy(ies)
  - clear description of data gathering procedures? Yes [✔] No [ ]
  - if "no," how could the description be improved?
  - description of gaining access? Yes [✔] No [ ]
  - discussion of time frame of data gathering? Yes [ ] No [✔]

j. Data Analysis Strategies

- description of the method(s) used? Yes [✔] No [   ]
- identification of categories or common elements found? Yes [✔] No [   ]
- report of the participants' response to the analysis? Yes [   ] No [✔]
- data analysis presented in a clear framework (identification of central themes and categories)? Yes [✔] No [   ]
- data presented in such a way that relationships between categories/themes are clear? Yes [✔] No [   ]
- analysis well supported by representative quotes/findings? Yes [✔] No [   ]
- provision of evidence as to how representative in the sample the various findings were? Yes [✔] No [   ]

k. Conclusions, Discussion, Implications, Suggestions for Further Study

- identification of limitations of study? Yes [✔] No [   ]
- specific limitations identified: Questioned whether health care professionals would have the same interpretation as "successful in self-care management" as the persons with diabetes
- discussion pertains to all significant findings? Yes [✔] No [   ]
- interpretive statements correspond with findings? Yes [✔] No [   ]
- examination of findings with existing body of knowledge? Yes [✔] No [   ]
- clear indication of directives for future research? Yes [✔] No [   ]
- If "yes," indicate directives identified: Investigation of variables that affect how and when individuals decide to assume control in self-care management; how health care professionals can assist individuals with diabetes to progress developmentally in relation to self-care management; how can this decision making, including reading the body, be taught to novice diabetics; how do novices make their decisions in comparison to the experts; variables that affect decision making; efficacy of a mentoring program in teaching novices to assume control in self-care management; accuracy of experts' decision making; research re men's experience and that of members of specific cultural groups.

Other Considerations/Thoughts:

- People who were diagnosed 30 years ago have a very different trajectory than those who are more recently diagnosed. Would the more recently diagnosed have the same experience in assuming control of their self-care management?

- Is one interview sufficient to capture the participant's experience?

- Do people with other chronic illnesses experience the same developmental changes in relation to assuming control of self-care management?

- What assumptions does the nomination method imply? For example, does the nomination by health care professionals mean that persons with diabetes are only expert if the professionals define them as such?

Decision to Include in Meta-Study:

Yes [✔] No   [ ] Undecided   [ ]   (explain below)

Appendix B: Table of Primary Research Features

Code Number	Authors	Publication Year	Chronic Disease(s)	Theoretical Orientation	Methodological Orientation	Major Findings (Take-Home Message)
001	Paterson & Sloan	1994	Diabetes	Self-care decision making	Interpretive Phenomenology	Decision to assume control of self-care management is critical to development of expertise in self-care.
002	LeMone	1991	Diabetes	Sexual function	Grounded Theory	Change in sexual function caused by diabetes leads to transformation of self.
003	Robinson	1990	Multiple sclerosis	Life trajectories	Narrative Analysis	Personal narrative is as significant in the life trajectory as are illness and sickness.
004	Thoman-Touet	1992	Unspecified chronic illness	Mental quality	Unspecified	Chronic illness has an impact on mental outlook and status.
005	Price	1988	Diabetes	Trajectory/ Uncertainty	Grounded Theory	A sequential trajectory is linked to one's ability to manage diabetes.

Appendix B *(Continued)*

Code Number	Authors	Publication Year	Chronic Disease(s)	Theoretical Orientation	Methodological Orientation	Major Findings (Take-Home Message)
006	Charmaz	1983	Various chronic diseases	Suffering/ Loss of self	Grounded Theory	Retrospective view of suffering as path to self-discovery and self-knowledge.
007	LeMone	1995	Diabetes	Roy's Adaptation Theory	Generic	Psychosexual changes affect the individual holistically.
008	Scambler & Hopkins	1986	Epilepsy	Stigma	Generic	(a) People with epilepsy fear and experience stigma. (b) Fear is more disruptive than "actual" stigma.
009	Williams	1984	Rheumatoid arthritis	Narrative reconstruction in illness	Narrative Analysis	The cause of illness may be attributable to science, morality, fact, value, or disease.
010	Stewart & Sullivan	1982	Multiple sclerosis	Illness behavior/Sick role	Generic	People with MS constantly negotiate order between physicians and selves.

REFERENCES

Aldag, R. J., & Stearns, T. M. (1998). Issues in research methodology. *Journal of Management, 14,* 253-276.

Alexander, J. C., & Colomy, P. (1992). Traditions and competition: Preface to a postpositivist approach to knowledge cumulation. In G. Ritzer (Ed.), *Meta-theorizing* (pp. 7-26). Newbury Park, CA: Sage.

Altheide, D. L., & Johnson, J. M. (1994). Criteria for assessing interpretive validity in qualitative research. In N. K. Denzin & Y. S. Lincoln (Eds.), *Handbook of qualitative research* (pp. 485-499). Thousand Oaks, CA: Sage.

Anderson, J. M. (1991). Reflexivity in fieldwork: Toward a feminist epistemology. *Image: Journal of Nursing Scholarship, 23*(2), 115-118.

Angen, M. J. (2000). Evaluating interpretive inquiry: Reviewing the validity debate and opening the dialogue. *Qualitative Health Research, 10,* 378-395.

Baker, C., Wuest, J., & Stern, P. (1992). Method slurring: The grounded theory/phenomenology example. *Journal of Advanced Nursing, 17,* 1355-1360.

Barroso, J., & Powell-Cope, G. (2000). Meta-synthesis of qualitative research on living with HIV infection. *Qualitative Health Research, 10,* 340-353.

Baszanger, I., & Dodier, N. (1998). Ethnography: Relating the part to the whole. In D. Silverman (Ed.), *Qualitative research: Theory, method, and practice* (pp. 8-23). London: Sage.

Bridge, M. J. (1986). *A phenomenological study of being a homosexual male who has been diagnosed with AIDS.* Unpublished doctoral dissertation, California School of Professional Psychology, Fresno.

Brookfield, S. D. (1991). The development of critical reflection in adulthood: Foundations of a theory of adult learning. *New Education, 13*(1), 39-48.

Brueggermann, W. (1977). *The land.* Philadelphia: Fortress.

Bryant, C. G. A. (1995). *Practical sociology: Post-empiricism and the reconstruction of theory and application.* Cambridge, MA: Polity.

Burke, S. O., Kaufmann, E., Costello, E., Wiskin, N., & Harrison, M. B. (1998). Stressors in families with a child with a chronic condition: An analysis of qualitative studies and a framework. *Canadian Journal of Nursing Research, 30*(1), 71-95.

Burns, N. (1989). Standards for qualitative research. *Nursing Science Quarterly, 2,* 44-52.

Butterfield, P. G. (1990). Thinking upstream: Nurturing a conceptual understanding of the societal context of health behavior. *Advances in Nursing Science, 12,* 1-8.

Caelli, K. (2000).The changing face of phenomenological research: Traditional and American phenomenology in nursing. *Qualitative Health Research, 10,* 366-377.

Carpenter, C. (1994). The experience of spinal cord injury: The individual's perspective—implications for rehabilitation practice. *Physical Therapy, 74,* 614-629.

Charmaz, K. (1983). Loss of self: A fundamental form of suffering in the chronically ill. *Sociology of Health and Illness, 5,* 168-195.

Charmaz, K., & Olesen, V. (1997). Ethnographic research in medical sociology: Its foci and distinctive contributions. *Sociological Methods & Research, 25,* 452-494.

Chinn, P., & Kramer, M. K. (1995). *Theory and nursing: A systematic approach* (4th ed.). St. Louis, MO: C. V. Mosby.

Cohen, B. P. (1994). Sociological theory: The half-full cup. In J. Hage (Ed.), *Formal theory in sociology* (pp. 66-83). Albany: State University of New York Press.

Conrad, P. (1990). Qualitative research on chronic illness: A commentary on method and conceptual development. *Social Science and Medicine, 30,* 1257-1263.

Cook, T. D., & Leviton, L. C. (1980). Reviewing the literature: A comparison of traditional methods with meta-analysis. *Journal of Personality, 48,* 449-472.

Cooper, H. M. (1982). Scientific guidelines for conducting integrative research reviews. *Review of Educational Research, 52,* 291-302.

Cooper, H. M. (1984). *The integrative research review: A systematic approach.* Beverly Hills, CA: Sage.

Cooper, H. M. (1986). On the social psychology of using research reviews: The case of desegregation and black achievement. In R. S. Feldman (Ed.), *The social psychology of education* (pp. 341-363). Cambridge, UK: Cambridge University Press.

Cooper, H. M. (1987). Literature searching strategies of integrative research reviewers: A first survey. *Knowledge: Creation, Diffusion, Utilization, 8,* 372-383.

Cooper, H. M., & Lindsay, J. J. (1998). Research synthesis and meta-analysis. In L. Bickman & D. J. Rog (Eds.), *Handbook of applied social research methods* (pp. 315-337). Thousand Oaks, CA: Sage.

Coward, D. D., & Lewis, F. M. (1993). The lived experience of self-transcendence in gay men with AIDS. *Oncology Nursing Forum, 20,* 1363-1368.

Crossley, M. (1998). "Sick role" or "empowerment"? The ambiguities of life with an HIV diagnosis. *Sociology of Health & Illness, 20,* 509-531.

Crotty, M. (1998). *The foundations of social research: Meaning and perspective in the research process.* London: Sage.

Cummings, K. M. (1987). Dilemmas in studying health as an individual phenomenon. In M. E. Duffy & N. J. Pender (Eds.), *Conceptual issues in health promotion: A report of proceedings of a Wingspread conference* (pp. 91-96). Indianapolis: Sigma Theta Tau.

Curtin, M., & Lubkin, I. M. (1990). What is chronicity? In I. M. Lubkin (Ed.), *Chronic illness: Impact and intervention* (2nd ed., pp. 2-20). Boston: Jones & Bartlett.

D'Antonio, P. (1997). Toward a history of research in nursing. *Nursing Research, 46,* 105-110.

Demas, P., Schoenbaum, E. E., Willis, T. A., Doll, L. S., & Klein, R. S. (1995). Stress, coping, and attitudes toward HIV treatment in injecting drug users: A qualitative study. *AIDS Education and Prevention, 7,* 429-442.

Denzin, N. K. (1989). *Interpretive interactionism.* Newbury Park, CA: Sage.

Diederiks, J. P. M., & Bal, R. M. (1997). Perspectives on patient career in chronic illness: Theoretical status and practical implications. *Sociological Focus, 30,* 167-175.

Dildy, S. M. P. (1992). *A naturalistic study of the nature, meaning, and impact of suffering in people with rheumatoid arthritis.* Unpublished doctoral dissertation, University of Texas, Austin.

Dluhy, N. M. (1995). Mapping knowledge in chronic illness. *Journal of Advanced Nursing, 21,* 1051-1058.

Dubos, R. (1965). *Man adapting.* New Haven, CT: Yale University Press.

Duldt, B., & Griffin, K. (1985). *Theoretical perspectives for nursing.* Boston: Little, Brown.

Engel, J. D., & Kuzel, A. J. (1992). On the idea of what constitutes good qualitative inquiry. *Qualitative Health Research, 2,* 504-510.

Erlandson, D. A., Harris, E. L., Skipper, B. L., & Allen, S. D. (1993). *Doing naturalistic inquiry: A guide to methods.* Newbury Park, CA: Sage.

Estabrooks, C. A., Field, P. A., & Morse, J. M. (1994). Aggregating qualitative findings: An approach to theory development. *Qualitative Health Research, 4,* 503-511.

Fawcett, J., & Downs, F. S. (1992) *The relationship of theory and research* (2nd ed.). Philadelphia: F. A. Davis.

Ferguson, P. M., Ferguson, D. L., & Taylor, S. J. (1992). Conclusion: The future of interpretivism in disability studies. In P. M. Ferguson, D. L. Ferguson, & S. J. Taylor (Eds.), *Interpreting disability: A qualitative reader* (pp. 295-302). New York: Teachers College Press.

Field, P. A., & Marck, P. (1994). *Uncertain motherhood: Negotiating risk in the childbearing years.* Thousand Oaks, CA: Sage.

Fielding, N. G., & Fielding, J. L. (1986). *Linking data.* Newbury Park, CA: Sage.

Flew, A. (1991). *Thinking about social thinking* (2nd ed.). New York: HarperCollins.

Frankel, R. M. (1999). Standards of qualitative research. In B. F. Crabtree & W. L. Miller (Eds.), *Doing qualitative research* (2nd ed.). Thousand Oaks, CA: Sage.

Frankish, C. J. (1998). Principles of authorship in health promotion research. *Canadian Journal of Public Health, 89,* 81-84.

Fuchs, S. (1992). Relativism and reflexivity in the sociology of scientific knowledge. In G. Ritzer (Ed.), *Meta-theorizing* (pp. 151-167). Newbury Park, CA: Sage.

Fuhrman, E. R., & Snizek, W. (1990). Neither proscience nor antiscience: Meta-sociology as dialogue. *Sociological Forum, 5,* 17-36.

Furfey, P. H. (1953). *The scope and method of sociology: A meta-sociological treatise.* New York: Cooper Square.

Gerhardt, U. (1990). Qualitative research on chronic illness: The issue and the story. *Social Science & Medicine, 30,* 1149-1159.

Glaser, B., & Strauss, A. (1967). *The discovery of grounded theory.* Chicago: Aldine.

Glass, G. V., Smith, M. L., & McGaw, B. (1981). *Meta-analysis in social research.* Beverly Hills, CA: Sage.

Goffman, E. (1963). *Stigma: Notes on the management of a spoiled identity.* Englewood Cliffs, NJ: Prentice Hall.

Grassie, W. (1996). Donna Haraway's meta-theory of science and religion: Cyborgs, Trickster, and Hermes. *Zygon, 31,* 285-304.

Gregory, D. M. (1994). *Narratives of suffering in the cancer experience.* Unpublished doctoral dissertation, University of Arizona, Tucson.

Guba, E. G., & Lincoln, Y. S. (1994). Competing paradigms in qualitative research. In N. K. Denzin & Y. S. Lincoln (Eds.), *Handbook of qualitative research* (pp. 105-117). Thousand Oaks, CA: Sage.

Hamalainen, J. (1989). Social pedagogy as a meta-theory of social work education. *International Social Work, 32,* 117-128.

Hammersley, M. (1995). Theory and evidence in qualitative research. *Quality and Quantity, 29,* 55-66.

Harding, S. (1987). *Feminism and methodology.* Bloomington: University of Indiana.

Helson, H. (1964). *Adaptation level theory.* New York: Harper & Row.

Heyman, I. (1996). Current paradigms in a new research domain: The case of nursing research on diabetes in Sweden. *Scandinavian Journal of Caring Science, 10,* 242-246.

Hinds, P. S., Vogel, R. J., & Clarke-Steffen, L. (1997). The possibilities and pitfalls of doing a secondary analysis of a qualitative data set. *Qualitative Health Research, 7,* 408-424.

Hutchinson, S. (1986). Grounded theory: The method. In P. Munhall & C. Oiler (Eds.), *Nursing research: A qualitative perspective* (pp. 109-130). Norwalk, CT: Appleton-Century-Crofts.

Jensen, L. A., & Allen, M. N. (1994). A synthesis of qualitative research in wellness-illness. *Qualitative Health Research, 4,* 349-369.

Jensen, L. A., & Allen, M. N. (1996). Meta-synthesis of qualitative findings. *Qualitative Health Research, 6,* 553-560.

Johnson, M. (1999). Observations on positivism and pseudoscience in qualitative nursing research. *Journal of Advanced Nursing, 30,* 67-73.

Kasper, A. S. (1994). A feminist, qualitative methodology: A study of women with breast cancer. *Qualitative Sociology, 17,* 263-281.

Kavale, K. A., & Glass, G. V. (1981). Meta-analysis and the integration of research in special education. *Journal of Learning Disabilities, 14,* 531-538.

Kearney, M. H. (1998). Truthful self-nurturing: A grounded formal theory of women's addiction recovery. *Qualitative Health Research, 8,* 495-512.

Kendall, J. (1991). *Human satisfaction and wellness in homosexual men with HIV infection: A grounded theory.* Unpublished doctoral dissertation, Georgia State University, Atlanta.

Knafl, K., & Breitmayer, B. (1991). Triangulation in qualitative research: Issues of conceptual clarity and purpose. In J. M. Morse (Ed.), *Qualitative nursing research: A contemporary dialogue* (pp. 209-218). Newbury Park, CA: Sage.

Kvale, S. (1995). The social construction of validity. *Qualitative Inquiry, 1,* 19-40.

Laskiwiski, S. (1990a). An ethnography of the spinal cord injury unit, Part 1. *AARN Newsletter, 46*(9), 14-15.

Laskiwiski, S. (1990b). An ethnography of the spinal cord injury unit, Part 2. *AARN Newsletter, 46*(10), 6-8.

Laskiwiski, S., & Morse, J. M. (1993). The patient with spinal cord injury: The modification of hope and expressions of despair. *Canadian Journal of Rehabilitation, 6*(3), 143-153.

Lawler, J. (1998). Phenomenologies as research methodologies for nursing: From philosophy to researching practice. *Nursing Inquiry, 5,* 104-111.

Lazarus, R. S., & Folkman, S. (1984). *Stress, appraisal, and coping.* New York: Springer.

LeMone, P. (1991). *Transforming: Patterns of sexual function in adults with insulin-dependent diabetes mellitus.* Unpublished doctoral dissertation, University of Alabama, Birmingham.

LeMone, P. (1995). Assessing psychosexual concerns in adults with diabetes: Pilot project using Roy's modes of adaptation. *Issues in Mental Health Nursing, 16,* 67-78.

Lenski, G. (1988). Rethinking macrosociological theory. *American Sociological Review, 57,* 1-15.

Lincoln, Y. S. (1995). Emerging criteria for quality in qualitative and interpretive research. *Qualitative Inquiry, 3,* 275-289.

Lincoln, Y. S., & Guba, E. G. (1985). *Naturalistic inquiry.* Beverly Hills, CA: Sage.

Lipson, J. G. (1989). The use of self in ethnographic research. In J. M. Morse (Ed.), *Qualitative nursing research: A contemporary dialogue* (pp. 61-75). Gaithersburg, MD: Aspen.

Loomis, M. E., & Conco, D. (1991). Patients' perceptions of health, chronic illness, and nursing diagnosis. *Nursing Diagnosis, 2,* 162-170.

May, K. A. (1994). Abstract knowing. In J. M. Morse (Ed.), *Critical issues in qualitative research methods* (pp. 10-21). Thousand Oaks, CA: Sage.

McKenna, H. P. (1997). Theory and research: A linkage to benefit practice. *International Journal of Nursing Studies, 34,* 431-437.

McKinlay, J. B. (1979). A case for refocusing upstream: The political economy of illness. In E. G. Jaco (Ed.), *Patients, physicians, and illness* (3rd ed., pp. 9-25). New York: Free Press.

McKinlay, J. B. (1992). Health promotion through healthy public policy: The contribution of complementary research methods. *Canadian Journal of Public Health/Revue Canadienne de Santé Publique, 83*(Suppl. 1), S11-S19.

McLaughlin, J., & Zeeberg, I. (1993). Self-care and multiple sclerosis: A view from two cultures. *Social Science & Medicine, 37*(3), 315-329.

Meleis, A. I. (1997). *Theoretical nursing: Development and progress* (3rd ed.). Philadelphia: J. B. Lippincott.

Messeri, P., Silverstein, M., & Litwak, E. (1993). Choosing optimal support groups: A review and reformulation. *Journal of Health and Social Behavior, 34,* 122-137.

Miles, M. B. (1983). Qualitative data as an attractive nuisance: The problem of analysis. In J. Van Maanen (Ed.), *Qualitative methodology* (pp. 117-134). Beverly Hills, CA: Sage.

Miles, M. B., & Huberman, A. M. (1994). *An expanded sourcebook: Qualitative data analysis* (2nd ed.). Thousand Oaks, CA: Sage.

Morse, J. M. (1994). Designing funded qualitative research. In N. Denzin & Y. Lincoln (Eds.), *Handbook of qualitative research* (pp. 220-235). Thousand Oaks, CA: Sage.

Morse, J. M. (1997). Responding to threats of integrity of self. *Advances in Nursing Science, 19,* 21-36.

Morse, J. M., & Bottorff, J. L. (1990). The use of ethnology in clinical nursing research. *Advances in Nursing Science, 12*(3), 53-64.

Morse, J. M., & Johnson, J. L. (Eds.). (1991). *The illness experience.* Newbury Park, CA: Sage.

Neufeld, M. (1994). Who's afraid of meta-theory? *Millennium, 23,* 387-393.

Noblit, G. W., & Hare, R. D. (1988). *Meta-ethnography: Synthesizing qualitative studies.* Newbury Park, CA: Sage.

O'Neill, M., & Pederson, A. P. (1992). Building a methods bridge between public policy analysis and healthy public policy. *Canadian Journal of Public Health/Revue Canadienne de Santé Publique, 83*(Suppl. 1), S25-S30.

Onyskiw, J. E. (1996). The meta-analytic approach to research integration. *Canadian Journal of Nursing Research, 28,* 69-85.

Orem, D. E. (1997). Views of human beings specific to nursing. *Nursing Science Quarterly, 10,* 26-31.

Orr, M. (1997). Sociological analyses of race and ethnicity since the 1950s: A sociology of sociology explanation for meta-theoretical shift. *Sociological Focus, 30,* 31-47.

Parsons, T. (1951). *The social system.* New York: Free Press.

Paterson, B., & Sloan, J. A. (1994). A phenomenological study of the decision making of individuals with long-standing diabetes. *Canadian Journal of Diabetes Care, 18*(4), 10-19.

Paterson, B., Thorne, S., Crawford, J., & Tarko, M. (1999). Living with diabetes as a transformational experience. *Qualitative Health Research, 9,* 786-802.

Paterson, B., Thorne, S., & Dewis, M. (1998). Adapting to and managing diabetes. *Image: Journal of Nursing Scholarship, 30,* 57-62.

Patton, M. Q. (1990). *Qualitative evaluation and research methods* (2nd ed.). Newbury Park, CA: Sage.

Pawson, R. (1989). *A measure for measures: A manifesto for empirical sociology.* London: Routledge.

Penrod, J., & Morse, J. M. (1997). Strategies for assessing and fostering hope: The hope assessment guide. *Oncology Nursing Forum, 24,* 1055-1063.

Price, M. J. (1988). *Perceived uncertainty associated with the management trajectory of a chronic illness—Diabetes mellitus.* Unpublished doctoral dissertation, University of California, San Francisco.

Ragsdale, D., Kotarba, J. A., & Morrow, J. R. (1992). Quality of life of hospitalized persons with AIDS. *Image: Journal of Nursing Scholarship, 24,* 259-265.

Ray, M. A. (1994). The richness of phenomenology: Philosophic, theoretic, and methodologic concerns. In J.M. Morse (Ed.), *Critical issues in qualitative research methods* (pp. 117-133). Thousand Oaks, CA: Sage.

Reason, P. (1996). Reflections on the purposes of human inquiry. *Qualitative Inquiry, 2,* 15-28.

Reeder, F. (1988). Hermeneutics. In B. Sarter (Ed.), *Paths to knowledge: Innovative research methods for nursing* (pp. 193-238). New York: National League for Nursing.

Richards, T. J., & Richards, L. (1994). Using computers in qualitative research. In N. K. Denzin & Y. S. Lincoln (Eds.), *Handbook of qualitative research* (pp. 445-462). Thousand Oaks, CA: Sage.

Richman, H. P (1983). *The adventure of reason.* Westport, CT: Greenwood.

Ritzer, G. (1990). Meta-theorizing in sociology. *Sociological Forum, 5,* 3-15.

Ritzer, G. (1991). *Meta-theorizing in sociology.* Lexington, MA: Lexington Books.

Ritzer, G. (1992a). Meta-theorizing in sociology: Explaining the coming of age. In G. Ritzer (Ed.), *Meta-theorizing* (pp. 7-26). Newbury Park, CA: Sage.

Ritzer, G. (1992b). *Sociological theory* (3rd ed.). New York: McGraw-Hill.

Ritzer, G. (1994). *Sociological beginnings: On the origin of key ideas in sociology.* New York: McGraw-Hill.

Robinson, I. (1990). Personal narratives, social careers, and medical courses: Analyzing life trajectories in autobiographies of people with multiple sclerosis. *Social Science & Medicine, 30,* 1173-1186.

Rodgers, B. L., & Cowles, K. V. (1993). The qualitative research audit trail: A complex collection of documentation. *Research in Nursing & Health, 16,* 219-226.

Sandelowski, M. (1986). The problem of rigor in qualitative research. *Advances in Nursing Science, 8,* 27-37.

Sandelowski, M. (1993a). Rigor or rigor mortis: The problem of rigor in qualitative research revisited. *Advances in Nursing Science, 16*(2), 1-8.

Sandelowski, M. (1993b). Theory unmasked: The uses and guises of theory in qualitative research. *Research in Nursing & Health, 16,* 213-218.

Sandelowski, M. (1995). Sample size in qualitative research. *Research in Nursing & Health, 18,* 179-183.

Sandelowski, M. (1997). "To be of use": Enhancing the utility of qualitative research. *Nursing Outlook, 45,* 125-132.

Sandelowski, M., Docherty, S., & Emden, C. (1997). Qualitative meta-synthesis: Issues and techniques. *Research in Nursing & Health, 20,* 365-371.

Scambler, G., & Hopkins, A. (1986). Being epileptic: Coming to terms with stigma. *Sociology of Health and Illness, 8,* 26-43.

Schreiber, R., Crooks, D., & Stern, P. N. (1997). Qualitative meta-analysis. In J. M. Morse (Ed.), *Completing a qualitative project: Details and dialogue* (pp. 311-326). Thousand Oaks, CA: Sage.

Selye, H. (1976). *The nature of adaptation: The stress of life.* New York: McGraw-Hill.

Sherwood, G. (1999). Meta-synthesis: Merging qualitative studies to develop nursing knowledge. *International Journal for Human Caring, 3*(1), 37-42.

Sherwood, G. D. (1997). Meta-synthesis of qualitative analyses of caring: Defining a therapeutic model of nursing. *Advanced Practice Nursing Quarterly, 3*(1), 32-42.

Silverman, D. (1998). The quality of qualitative health research: The open-ended interview and its alternatives. *Social Sciences in Health, 4*(2), 104-118.

Smith, D. E. (1990). *Conceptual practices of power: A feminist sociology of knowledge.* London: Routledge.

Statham, A., Mauksch, H. O., & Miller, E. M. (1988). Women's approach to work: The creation of knowledge. In A. Statham, E. M. Miller, & H. O. Mauksch (Eds.), *The worth of women's work: A qualitative synthesis* (pp. 3-9). Albany: State University of New York Press.

Steeves, R. H., Kahn, D. L., & Cohen, M. Z. (1996). Asking substantive theory questions of naturalistically derived data. *Western Journal of Nursing Research, 18,* 209-212.

Stern, P., & Harris, C. (1985). Women's health and the self-care paradox: A model to guide self-care readiness—clash between the client and nurse. *Health Care for Women International, 6,* 151-163.

Stern, P., & Pyles, S. (1986). Using grounded theory methodology to study women's culturally based decisions about health. In P. Stern (Ed.), *Women, health, and culture* (pp. 1-23). Washington, DC: Hemisphere.

Stern, P. N. (1994). Eroding grounded theory. In J. M. Morse (Ed.), *Critical issues in qualitative research methods* (pp. 212-223). Thousand Oaks, CA: Sage.

Stewart, D. C., & Sullivan, T. J. (1982). Illness behavior and the sick role in chronic disease: The case of multiple sclerosis. *Social Science & Medicine, 16,* 1397-1404.

Strauss, A. (1995). Notes on the nature and development of general theories. *Qualitative Inquiry, 1,* 7-18.

Strauss, A., & Corbin, J. (1990). *Basics of qualitative research.* Newbury Park, CA: Sage.

Strauss, A. L., & Glaser, B. G. (1975). *Chronic illness and the quality of life.* St. Louis, MO: C. V. Mosby.

Szabo, V., & Strang, V. R. (1997). Secondary analysis of qualitative data. *Advances in Nursing Science, 20,* 66-74.

Szmatka, J., & Lovaglia, M. J. (1996). The significance of method. *Sociological Perspectives, 39,* 393-415.

Szmatka, J., Lovaglia, M. J., & Mazur, J. (1996). The importance of method in development of sociological theory: Modification of conception of cumulative development of sociological knowledge by Berger, Wagner, and Zelditch. *Studia Socjologiczne, 2,* 55-85.

Thoman-Touet, S. K. (1992). *A qualitative study of the effect of chronic illness on marital quality.* Unpublished doctoral dissertation, Iowa State University, Ames.

Thorne, S. (1994). Secondary analysis in qualitative research: Issues and implications. In J. Morse (Ed.), *Critical issues in qualitative research methods* (pp. 263-279). Thousand Oaks, CA: Sage.

Thorne, S. (1997). The art (and science) of critiquing qualitative research. In J. M. Morse (Ed.), *Completing a qualitative project: Details and dialogue* (pp. 117-132). Thousand Oaks, CA: Sage.

Thorne, S., Kirkham, S. R., & MacDonald-Emes, J. (1997). Focus on qualitative methods: Interpretive description—A noncategorical qualitative alternative for developing nursing knowledge. *Research in Nursing and Health, 20,* 169-177.

Thorne, S. E. (1991). Methodological orthodoxy in qualitative nursing research: Analysis of the issues. *Qualitative Health Research, 1,* 178-199.

Thorne, S. E., & Paterson, B. (1998). Shifting images of chronic illness. *Image: Journal of Nursing Scholarship, 30,* 173-178.

Thorne, S. E., & Robinson, C. A. (1988). Health care relationships: The chronic illness perspective. *Research in Nursing and Health, 11,* 293-300.

Weinstein, D., & Weinstein, M. A. (1992). The postmodern discourse of meta-theory. In G. Ritzer (Ed.), *Meta-theorizing* (pp. 135-150). Newbury Park, CA: Sage.

Williams, G. (1984). The genesis of chronic illness: Narrative reconstruction. *Sociology of Health and Illness, 6,* 175-200.

Wolcott, H. F. (1990). On seeking—and rejecting—validity in qualitative research. In E. W. Eisner & A. Peshkin (Eds.), *Qualitative inquiry in education: The continuing debate* (pp. 121-153). New York: Teachers College Press.

Wolcott, H. F. (1995). *The art of fieldwork.* Thousand Oaks, CA: Altamira.

Zhao, S. (1991). Meta-theory, meta-method, meta-data-analysis: What, why, and how? *Sociological Perspectives, 34,* 377-390.

Zhao, S. (1996). The beginning of the end or the end of the beginning? The theory construction movement revisited. *Sociological Forum, 11,* 305-318.

NAME INDEX

SUBJECT INDEX

ABOUT THE AUTHORS

BARBARA L. PATERSON, RN, PhD, is Associate Professor in the School of Nursing at the University of British Columbia, Canada. She teaches and conducts research about chronic illness in general, but much of her work has been in the field of diabetes self-care. The focus of her research has been how individuals with long-standing chronic illness learn to make decisions about what works for them in their disease management even though sometimes those decisions are contrary to what health care professionals have advised.

SALLY E. THORNE, RN, PhD, is Professor in the School of Nursing at the University of British Columbia, Canada. Her research has focused on the experience of receiving health care for chronic illness, and she has conducted an extensive program of research on topics related to cancer and various other chronic diseases. She has focused particularly on the social context in which chronic health challenges are experienced, the impact of various health service delivery processes on quality of life, and the role that communication plays in the experience of being ill.

CONNIE CANAM, RN, PhD candidate, is Assistant Professor in the School of Nursing at the University of British Columbia, Canada. Her research focuses on chronic illness in children, with a particular interest in parents of children with chronic health problems. Currently, she teaches courses in the foundations of nursing practice, nursing ethics, and health policy.

CAROL JILLINGS, RN, PhD, is Associate Professor in the School of Nursing at the University of British Columbia, Canada. She teaches in the areas of theory development, concept analysis, and curriculum. Her area of interest is cardiac rehabilitation and health promotion, particularly with respect to nontraditional populations.